MARIO
LEMIEUX

BEST THERE EVER WAS

BY DAVE MOLINARI, RON COOK AND CHUCK FINDER

FROM THE SPORTS PAGES OF THE PITTSBURGH POST-GAZETTE

MIKE BYNUM, EDITOR

MACMILLAN CANADA
TORONTO

Acknowledgements

RESEARCH ASSISTANCE:
Fritz Huysman, Jim Barger, Danny Palmer, Laurie Hanson, Curt Chandler, Matt Kennedy, Tim Rozgonyi, Lizabeth Gray and the Pittsburgh Post-Gazette sports staff; Allsport Photography USA; The Gazette (of Montreal, Quebec) photo department; Wide World Photo; The Canadian Press photo department; the National Hockey League; and the Pittsburgh Penguins.

First published in Canada in 1997 by Macmillan Canada.

Canadian Cataloguing in Publication Data
Molinari, Dave
Mario Lemieux: Best There Ever Was
ISBN 0-7715-7551-3
1. Lemieux, Mario, 1965- 2. Hockey players- Canada- Biography.
I. Cook, Ron. II. Finder, Chuck. III. Bynum, Mike. IV. Title.
GV848.5.L45M64 1997 796.962'092 C97-931062-8

COVER AND BOOK DESIGN:
Joe Zeff, New York.
Typefaces: Citadel, FB Californian.

A Masters Press book.

CONTENTS

IEUX

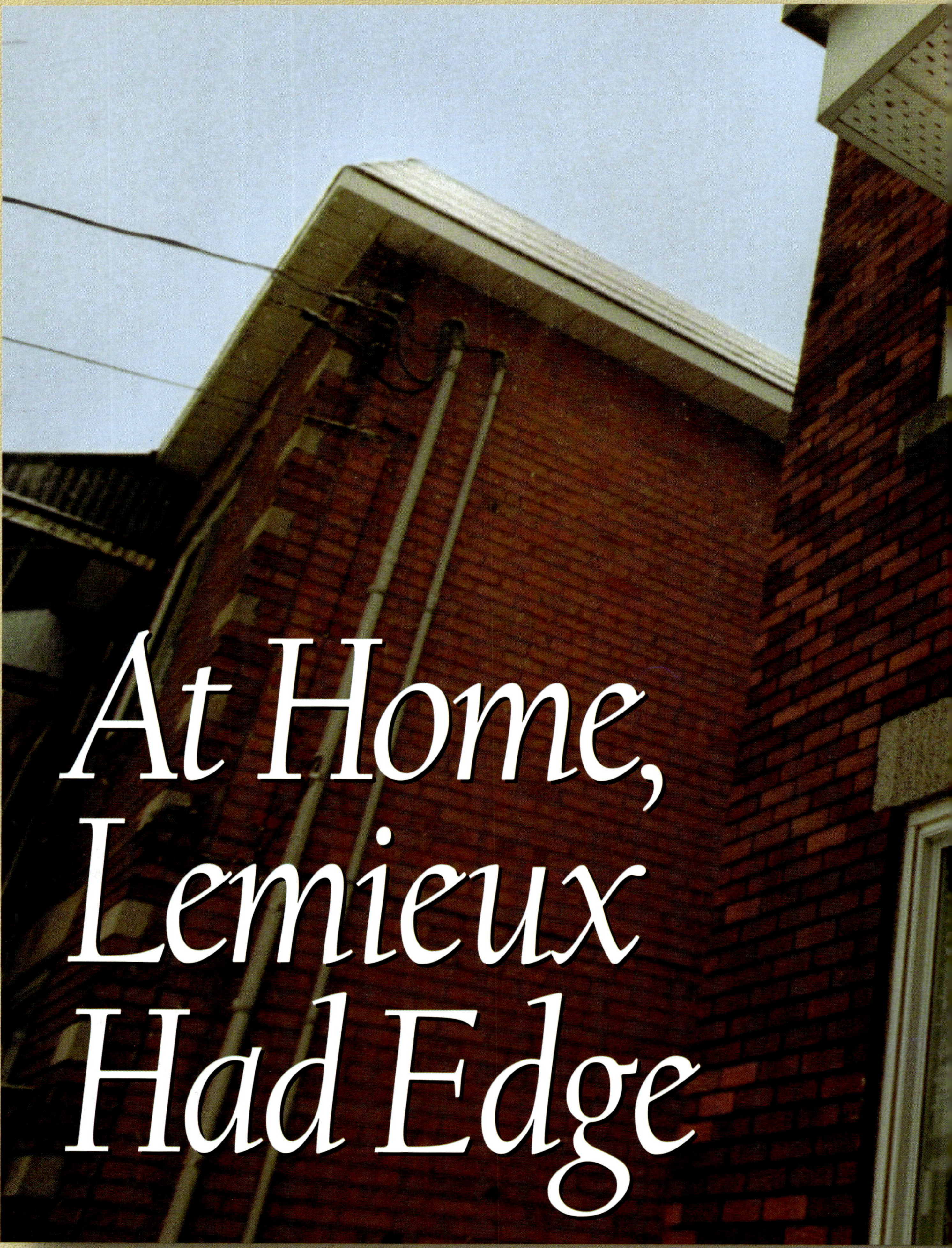

At Home, Lemieux Had Edge

CHAPTER 1

The Prodigy

Lemieux was the No. 1 junior player in Canada in 1983 and 1984. Among the trophies and articles decorating his bedroom in 1983 was a photograph of Wayne Gretzky. Another icon that still hangs on the wall in his parents' house: Lemieux's first pair of fitted skates.

BY CHUCK FINDER
Pittsburgh Post-Gazette

THE BIRTHPLACE OF THIS legend wasn't a frozen pond in Canada. It wasn't one of Canada's cold, concrete rinks. ¶ It was a basement. ¶ In fact, it was the basement of the simple, two-floor rowhouse at 6700 Rue Jogues in Montreal where the boy honed his hockey skills, where he began his scoring sojourn. The venue was symbolic: Just as he would time and again, with junior Laval and professional Pittsburgh, Mario Lemieux began his ascent from the cellar. ¶ Before he glided past defensemen and made the puck dance, he deked around columns in the family basement. Before he banked pucks off goaltenders and goal posts, he plinked them off his mother's

The Prodigy

piano. Before he triumphantly raised his stick to the glee of thousands, he ripped the hell out of Jean-Guy and Pierrette Lemieux's ceiling.

He shoots. He scores. He exults.

Oops.

"We had to change the ceiling a few times," their youngest son recalls with a smile.

There was Mario, Richard (his elder by a year) and Alain (older by three more). They played with big spoons and ketchup-bottle caps. They played with plastic pucks and wooden hockey sticks. They played and played and played in that basement. And Jean-Guy and Pierrette just kept replacing the ceiling and repairing the tile floor and wearing Band-Aids whenever tinkling the chipped piano keys.

But the Lemieuxs knew. From that basement arose two National Hockey League players, a far better rate than any other basement on Rue Jogues, in blue-collar Ville Emard, in West-End Montreal, in possibly all of Quebec. Alain went on to play for the Quebec Nordiques, the St. Louis Blues, even a game with the Penguins. Mario went on to magnificence.

On a snowy March day decades later, Mario Lemieux sat in the same basement only a few games before the end of an NHL career that saw him win — take a deep breath — three Hart trophies (for MVP), four Lester B. Pearson awards (for the best player, as chosen by his peers), six Art Ross trophies (for a scoring championship), two Conn Smythe trophies (for playoff MVP) and two Stanley Cups. He and the family waxed nostalgic. The ceiling. The piano. The goals. The marathon games, brother against brother, every Lemieux for himself.

So when did the boys do their homework?

"Between periods," said Richard.

Doesn't matter, adds Pierrette: "It's a good thing they played hockey and

GRETZKY WAS TEASING LEMIEUX'S AGENTS, "YOU TELL YOUR KID HE'D BETTER WAKE UP EARLY IF HE'S GOING TO TAKE OVER FOR ME."

didn't study."

A good thing for all of hockey, because the cellar produced a man who knew no ceiling.

MONTREAL BEGAN buzzing about the little Lemieux around 1971, when he was a mere 6 years old. Alain's Pee Wee team was playing an exhibition when the coach summoned the little brother from the stands. The boy was just a Mosquito division player — or, in the French pronunciation of his father, a *Mah-SKEE-toe*. Still, folks knew of the little Lemieux who needed no chair to support him when learning to skate on the two rinks behind St. Jean de Matha on Rue Dumas, a couple of blocks from Jogues.

Mario the Mosquito had a goal and an assist that day against Pee Wee players two and three years older. Not too shabby for a kid who started out a defenseman. "I used to go back and get the puck," he recalls, "and wheel it."

His skates and his magical stick carved both Quebec ice and a reputation. In one account, at age 8, he possessed such a nasty slapshot that he once injured a goalie. On the next breakaway, the goalie high-tailed it into the corner to hide, and Lemieux had what amounted to the first of many empty-net goals.

He glided through the Mosquito, Atom, Pee Wee and Bantam age divisions. He played on the powerhouse Ville Emard Hurricanes along with future NHL players J.J. Daigneault and Sylvain Cote.

"Everyone was talking about him," says Steve Finn, later a Laval teammate and an opposing NHL defenseman.

Mario, a center wearing No. 27 — after big brother Alain — grew tall. So did the stories. Eventually, the coach of the Montreal Canadiens, Scotty Bowman, decided to see for himself. Bowman came away duly impressed.

The center was 13 then.

"The first time I ever heard of Mario Lemieux was through Scotty Bowman, indirectly," said Bob Perno, the Montreal-based half of the agent tandem — with Toronto-based Gus Badali — that represented Wayne Gretzky. "He was quoted in the paper, 'I have seen a young man named Mario Lemieux play hockey. He will be a star in the NHL.' The name stayed in my head.

"A couple years later, I went to a hockey school in the summer at McGill University. I looked down on the ice and I saw this big kid out there skating through everybody. I asked, 'Who is that guy?'

" 'That's Mario Lemieux.'

"I just fell in love with him. I saw great things for him the first day I saw him. That night, I called Gus and said, 'This guy is good. This guy is another Wayne.'

"He said, 'Don't even say that.' I said, 'But he's another Wayne, only bigger.' "

Soon enough, Perno and Badali were representing a 15-year-old center drafted with the first pick overall in the Quebec Major Junior Hockey League — by cellar-dwelling Laval. Gretzky, by then a two-time NHL scoring champion, was teasing his agents, "You tell your kid he'd better wake up early if he's going to take over from me."

In the summer of 1981, before Lemieux reported to Laval in northeast Montreal, he was riding a train with Perno. They were en route to Gretzky's annual golf outing in Brantford, Ontario, when Perno raised the question of The Next Great One's jersey number. Perno remembers it this way:

"I want to wear 27," Lemieux said. Again, big brother Alain's number.

"Well, family's family," Perno replied. "But you both have careers.

Lemieux raised Laval from the cellar of the Quebec Major Junior Hockey League to one of Canada's best. By the end of his career there, NHL scouts scrambled for seats in the building where the team played.

They should be separate and distinct."

"What number do you think I should wear, then?"

"Mario, I think you're going to be one of the best players of all time. To me, the best player of all time is Wayne Gretzky."

"OK, I'll take 99."

"No, don't do that. I don't think it's fair to Wayne, and it's not fair to you. There's only one Wayne Gretzky, and only one Mario Lemieux."

"So what should I do?" Lemieux asked.

"Why not 66?" Perno said. "It's 99 upside down. People will compare you to Wayne, but they won't criticize you."

Half a Lemieux lifetime later, Perno says, "In a way, it was a soft comparison to Wayne. But it was more of a marketing thing at the time."

Le Soixante Six captured attention, to be sure.

Centre Sportif Laval was a drafty place before the lanky center from Ville Emard arrived. "The building was empty; you could hear flies buzz around," Perno says. Soon, the barn would be full, 4,000 people, cars parked down past the College Francais and the grey-stone federal prison. The only time during Lemieux's three seasons the place felt drafty was between periods, when the doors were opened to allow all the smoke to clear. From cigarettes, that is, not his blazing shots.

That first season he had 30 goals and, appropriately enough, 66 assists. Laval climbed from the cellar, but the lanky center wanted more. In a transaction later forgotten, the Montreal Canadiens sent Pierre Larouche to woebegone Hartford for the Whalers' 1982 first-round pick, hoping against hope that it would land the boy from Ville Emard.

The next season, deep in a scoring race with the United States' Pat LaFontaine of Verdun, Lemieux left the Quebec league to play for Team Canada in the prestigious World Junior Championships.

Defensive-minded Dave King, the coach of that Canadian national team, benched the offensive center for three games, and Lemieux vowed to stay home the next winter.

"Pat LaFontaine overtook him in the scoring race, his team lost in the playoffs, and Mario didn't perform as well as he did in the first half of the year," Perno says. "At the end of the year, he said, 'Bob, if they invite me next year, I'm not going. I promised Mr. (Claude) Fournel (the Laval team owner) a Memorial Cup appearance. I have one more year left. I'm not going to jeopardize that for anything.' "

He kept his word.

It created quite a stir, and Lemieux went to court over it.

The Quebec league maintained that Lemieux had a contract and a duty to play for his country. The kid argued that he wanted to stay with Laval, win the scoring title, and enjoy Christmas with his family and countless relatives around Ville Emard. The league tried to suspend him from the 1984 all-star game and more, and the case went to provincial court. The kid won.

"Mario seemed to have a knack for stirring up controversy," Perno says. "But Mario, even at that young age, was so strong in character. He had an unbelievable maturity. Nothing bothered him. He took the pressure and converted it into success. He turned that team into a Memorial Cup contender. He broke all the records."

Those long, gliding strides and puck-dangling magic served him well that third Laval season. Finn, a native of the city, remembers seeing Lemieux play when the center was 17 and then again when he was 18. "What a difference," Finn says. "That last year, he was untouchable."

Torturing goaltenders such as Granby's Patrick Roy, Lemieux had so many goals, so many points, that he was bearing down on the Quebec league records of NHL Hall of Famer Guy Lafleur. He had a 61-game scoring streak. Amazingly, adds teammate Michel Mongeau, "We had a 70-game schedule."

Lemieux dominated, and he thoroughly enjoyed it. Laval lost only 16 of those 70 games. Mongeau continues, "He wanted to be the best. But he never made us feel bad about it. Still, you knew he always wanted the puck."

In the regular-season final in 1983-84, with NHL scouts already scrambling for seats in the filled building, Perno invited Gretzky and Edmonton teammate Paul Coffey from Montreal to see local hockey history.

"He needed three goals to break Guy Lafleur's record," Finn said. "He didn't get any the first period. In the locker room, we were saying, 'C'mon Mario, wake up.' He said, 'Lotsa time. Lotsa time.'

"Sure enough, he did it."

Lemieux scored six goals that night, to go with five assists. He had his picture taken with Gretzky — or was it that Gretzky had his picture taken with him?

Le Soixante Six finished with a league-record 133 goals and 282 points and the enduring respect of one Eddie Johnston.

Johnston was the general manager of the cellar-dwelling Pittsburgh Penguins. At the time of Lemieux's record-setting night, the Penguins were battling the New Jersey Devils for last place. They secured that slot, and the subsequent No. 1 draft choice, after Johnston traded defenseman Randy Carlyle to Winnipeg for trinkets and beads, and he shipped young netminder Roberto Romano to the minors. Romano's replacement, Vincent Tremblay, leaked in two goals per period. The Penguins lost 15 of their final 18 games, including their last, and clinched that first pick. Clinched *Le Magnifique*.

Not that they were trying to or anything.

A native of Montreal's West End, Johnston likewise had heard talk of this Lemieux kid for a half-dozen years. Johnston spent the final two months of that 1983-84 junior season following the lanky center. He, too, was there that record-setting night.

"He could just do things with a puck that were unbelievable," Johnston says. "Unbelievable."

The draft took place in Lemieux's hometown, at the Montreal Forum, where Jean-Guy and Pierrette had

Lemieux tallied 11 points — six goals and five assists — in his final regular-season game of junior hockey for Laval.

MINNESOTA GM LOU NANNE OFFERED ALL 12 OF HIS TEAM'S SELECTIONS FOR THE RIGHT TO TAKE LEMIEUX AS THE FIRST PICK OF THE '84 DRAFT. QUEBEC OFFERED ANY OR ALL OF THE THREE STATSNYS — MARION, PETER AND ANTON. JOHNSTON TOLD THEM, IN THESE EXACT WORDS,

"STICK IT IN YOUR EAR."

"TALK ABOUT A GUY WHO SAVED THE FRANCHISE. THERE'S NO DOUBT ABOUT THAT."

Canadiens season tickets. Penguins management had begun contract talks with agents Perno and Badali. But there were rumors of trades, and there existed tangible doubt among Penguins types.

This, after all, was a franchise that traded away top-12 picks in six of the previous nine years, that drafted two Quebecois in all that time. The Penguins flopped with Pierre Larouche, allowing celebrity to swallow a budding superstar. They had endured the tragic death of another budding Francophone star, Michel Briere, in 1971. WEEP was an appropriate affiliate for a team that lost more often than it won in 13 of 17 seasons.

Minnesota GM Lou Nanne offered Johnston all 12 of the North Stars' draft picks for the right to select Lemieux with the first choice of the 1984 NHL Entry Draft. Quebec offered any combination of three Statsnys — Marion, Peter and Anton. All three, even. Johnston told them, in these exact words, "Stick it in your ear."

"I was emphatic I wasn't going to trade him," Johnston recalls. "But there were some people here who thought, 'Maybe we should take a couple players who could get us into the playoffs.' But that would cheat the fans here, I said.

"It really wasn't a hard decision."

On draft day, Johnston practiced his French, announced Lemieux as *Le Soixante Six*, and the lanky center did nothing but stand and salute the crowd. He and his agents were unhappy with contract negotiations. He refused the customary walk to the Penguins table and the donning of the selecting team's sweater. In a picture that hangs still in Jean-Guy and Pierrette's hallway, the same hallway where their three sons were allowed to skate on snow packed on top of indestructible carpet, the suit-wearing Mario is flanked by Kirk Muller in New Jersey's sweater and Ed Olczyk in Chicago's. "I am not going to their table because the Penguins do not want me badly enough," Lemieux was quoted as saying then.

He stirred controversy again. Canadian papers chastised him for the move. "Lemieux Behaving Like a Petulant Prima Donna," fairly screamed a Toronto *Globe and Mail* headline. A Penguins fan watching the draft at a Civic Arena ceremony fairly screamed as well: "I won't sign (for season tickets) until Lemieux signs."

Within a fortnight, Lemieux was signed, sealed and delivered. *Le Magnifique.* The savior of a franchise.

Sure, he scored on his first shift, his first shot, against Boston's Pete Peeters. But he didn't score another goal for another 10 games. The Flightless Waterfowl started 6-14-3. Oops.

Le Magnifique learned that his supporting cast left a distinct aroma. He also learned that, unlike any other level of hockey before, he couldn't dominate and carry a team. Especially a team of Gary Risslings and Todd Charlesworths and Mitch Lamoreauxs and Roger Belangers. Still, the rookie was able to turn a 28-year-old minor-leaguer named Warren Young into a 40-goal scorer and himself into a 43-goal, 100-point scorer. Only two other rookies in NHL history had ever scored as many. He won the Calder Trophy as rookie of the year.

"That was all the talk in the locker room: Mario, Mario, Mario," recalls Joey Mullen, an opponent with St. Louis and Calgary before becoming a teammate in 1990. "That was the whole game plan."

Attendance nearly doubled that first season, yet owner Edward DeBartolo talked about moving the team, possibly to Hamilton, Ontario. The real-estate and mall magnate groused about losing millions and how a hockey team was a bad investment. To sell tickets, the Penguins dangled *Le Magnifique* in front of the Pittsburgh populace. "Basically," Tom Rooney, then the vice president of advertising, would admit later, "we held him over people's heads."

The Penguins stayed, Lemieux displayed even more promise (141 points the next season and 107 in 63 games the following), and people began filling the Arena seats to 90-percent-plus capacity.

"Without Lemieux," Edmonton coach Glen Sather would say, "they pack up the team and move to another city."

Adds Johnston says, "Talk about a guy who saved the franchise. There's no doubt about that."

Oh, yes, the kid stirred controversy again. He played for Canada in the springtime World Championships his rookie season, then skipped the next couple years. He was more into golf than the foreign intrigue of battling the Big Red Machine that was Russia.

Ever the homebody, a boy who insulated himself like Ville Emard with tight rows of family and friends, Lemieux played his Nintendo, lived with longtime girlfriend Nathalie Asselin, tinkered with golf. It was a difficult transition indeed, coming to a foreign country with a foreign currency and a foreign language.

The kid became a millionaire, yet what eluded him was a pedestal of his own, international acclaim, or acclaim beyond Montreal and Pittsburgh even. His slow, gliding style of skating was judged as laziness. His defensive ability was questioned.

Bill Clement, player-turned-broadcaster, was quoted in the *Post-Gazette*: "You never see him in a do-or-die situation where he seems to want to die for it. You don't visualize a picture of a soldier with a bloody bandage wrapped around his head, his arm in a sling, uniform torn off his body, struggling to get back into battle, do you?"

Clement would have seen it if only he had looked harder.

THE BASEMENT WITH his brothers was where he was weaned. But the Canada Cup alongside Gretzky and the game's stars was where he matured.

Lemieux toiled on a Team Canada line with Gretzky and topped all scorers in this world-class tournament with 11 goals. He scored three consecutive goals, including the overtime winner, in a Game 2 that many puckheads consider one of the finest every contested. Most important, Lemieux learned about stardom, about the price of success.

At long last, he sported the captain's "C" with the Penguins. He scored a dramatic, from-his-keister, overtime goal at Washington in a must-win game that March. He tallied 70 goals, an NHL high. He shoved the Pen-

Lemieux poses with his parents, Jean-Guy (left) and Pierrette, upon receiving the Hart Trophy and Art Ross Trophy in 1996.

guins to a winning record for the first time in nine winters — although that still wasn't good enough to make the playoffs. Just as vital to his esteem and his rank in the hockey constellation, Lemieux won the scoring title (168 points) and was awarded the MVP Hart Trophy.

Lemieux scored an even more amazing 85 goals and 199 points the next season, 1989-90, the most prolific year by anyone not named Gretzky. That season ended in disappointment, too: The first Penguins playoffs in too long, and they fritter away a 3-2, second-round lead against Philadelphia. Then he was stiffed at the awards ceremony: no Hart Trophy.

The team improving only marginally, Penguins administrators began discarding coaches and general managers like old skates. Bob Berry, then Pierre Creamer, then Gene Ubriaco. Johnston, then Tony Esposito. Ubriaco, for one, began blaming the lanky center for his December 1989 exit, saying that coaching Lemieux and ex-Edmonton defenseman Coffey was like "trying to teach a shark table manners."

Craig Patrick entered that 1989-90 season, and Lemieux exited with an aching back — amid a 46-game scoring streak, second-longest in NHL history. He would play one game in the next 10 months.

Patrick was amazed at the captain's courage. Lemieux came back after a six-week hiatus to try to help the Penguins reach the 1990 playoffs with a season-finale victory, but failed.

No one should have been surprised by his desire, Perno says. He had seen this before: Lemieux virtually with an arm in a sling, struggling to get back into battle.

"I remember one time he was playing Midget AAA — he was 14, 15," the agent recalls. "It was the playoffs. I think they were down by a couple goals and it was late in the third period. Some guy slashed him on the arm; I thought he broke it. Big time. The trainer came out and said, 'There's no way he's going back out there.' A couple minutes later, he came out of the dressing room, he scores three goals and they win the game.

"Afterward, he takes his sweater off, and there's a lump on his forearm the size of a baseball. What they did was take his elbow pad and tape it over the lump. And he went out and scored three goals and they won.

"He's got incredible will. Incredible will."

CAPTAIN COMEBACK HE became.

There was back surgery that caused him to miss 50 games to start 1990-91. He ended the season with the

Conn Smythe Trophy as playoff MVP with 44 points and the Stanley Cup in his suburban Mt. Lebanon swimming pool.

There was the death of beloved Coach Badger Bob Johnson, more Lemieux backache, a brief strike and a wicked playoff slash from the New York Rangers' Adam Graves in 1991-92. He ended the season with another Conn Smythe Trophy and another Stanley Cup.

There was the most courageous comeback of all in 1992-93 — from cancer.

A lump in his neck was examined, and the 27-year-old man was diagnosed as having Hodgkin's disease. It had killed a relative. Two other family members battled cancer. He cried so much on his way home from the doctor it took him a half-hour to tell Nathalie the news.

Then came that incredible will.

After the month-long radiation treatments, *Le Magnifique* was back on the ice, chasing Pat LaFontaine for another scoring title.

"I remember the day of his last treatment," teammate Kevin Stevens would say later. "He got (to Philadelphia) about 4 o'clock in the afternoon and went out there and played."

Lemieux scored a goal that night. In his final 20 regular-season games, sapped and out of shape, Lemieux nonetheless had a remarkable 30 goals and 56 points.

He won more hardware: the Pearson, the Hart, and finally, the Masterton Trophy — awarded for perseverance, sportsmanship and dedication to hockey. Yeah, he scored that hat trick.

"The moment I found out I had cancer really changed my life and changed my outlook on life," Lemieux says. "I knew my health was No. 1 and my family was right up there. Hockey really took a back seat, whereas, before the cancer, hockey was No. 1 in my life — including over my family."

Lemieux takes the ice in March 1997 in his last regular-season game in his hometown of Montreal.

When he took a leave of absence in 1994-95, after two back surgeries and the Hodgkin's and the general fatigue from radiation treatments, he really didn't believe he would return to the ice.

"Nobody could have blamed Mario if he said, 'The hell with it,' and walked away, all the things he's been through," said teammate Ron Francis.

Lemieux allowed himself to climb from the cellar one last time, having worked out in the basement of his home during that off-year and ascending to the top of the NHL again.

"I don't know if I would have had the dedication, the endurance, the will to do what he's done," says Tom Plasko, his masseur, workout partner, prodder. "I saw changes every day in his attitude. You'd start to see it in his eyes; he was excited."

This was a radical departure. Lemieux's idea of off-season conditioning was golf and sleep. The captain once teased Francis that his preparation for training camp was to skip French fries with his club sandwich. In his rookie training camp, he struggled with weightlifting and distance running to the point where the Penguins worried about their investment — before he took the ice. Once he hit the frozen slab, he was magnificent almost immediately. "He'd take off the summer completely," recalls Perno. "He just didn't think that he needed (conditioning) because he'd pick up in September where he left in April."

This time, pushing 30 and pulling behind him emotional and physical scars, Lemieux was in shape, free of back pain and ready for another dra-

After being battered in a game, Lemieux receives a back massage from his therapist, Tom Plasko.

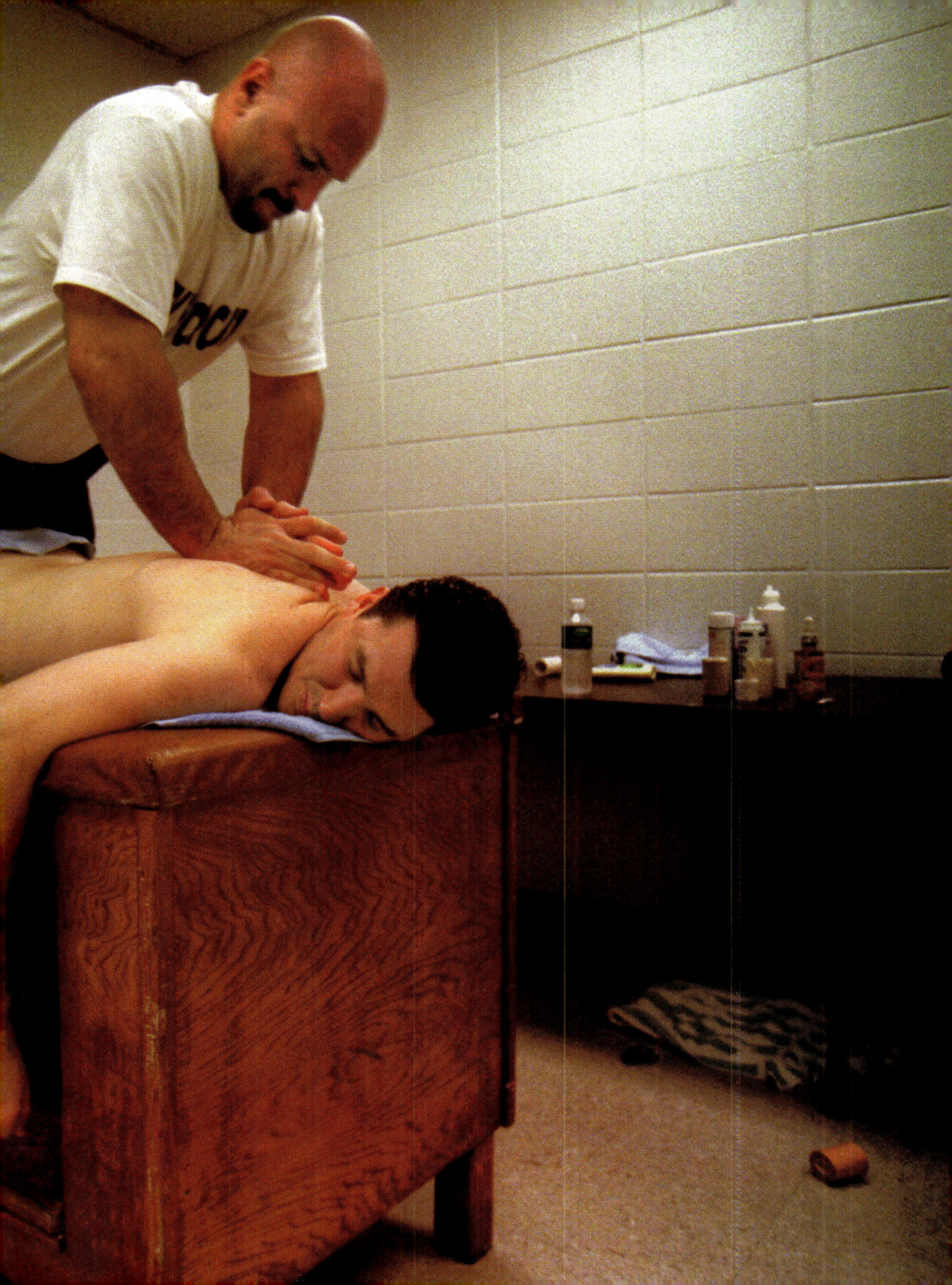

"NOT TAKING ANYTHING AWAY FROM GRETZKY, BUT IF MARIO HADN'T BEEN SICK, HE COULD HAVE AVERAGED 200 POINTS A YEAR."

Lemieux leaves the ice after his final game — a playoff-ending loss to the Philadelphia Flyers on April 26, 1997.

He brought the Penguins within one victory of the 1996 Stanley Cup finals. He won two more NHL scoring titles. He made the puck dance again.

Like Michael Jordan, he realized that age and game mileage caused the skills to erode a tad. "The last two years were a struggle, trying to play the way I used to in the past and not being able to challenge players one-on-one," Lemieux says. "It's something that is very frustrating because I've been able to do that for so many years."

Still, he played 70 games each of the final two seasons — something he accomplished in just four of his previous 10 seasons.

At the end of the 1996-97 season, he puts away that wand of a stick after weaving his magic into the top six of all-time NHL goal-scorers. He leaves the game after punctuating his final homecomings with a three-goal third period and a two-goal third period his last two trips into Montreal. He leaves the first NHL player to average two points per game through a career. He leaves after transforming cellar-dwelling Pittsburgh into a perennial playoff participant.

"Not taking anything away from Gretzky," says Johnston, who coached Lemieux most of the last two seasons, "but if Mario hadn't been sick, he could have averaged 200 points a year. Or there's no telling what he could have done."

"Looking back, I've pretty much done it all," Lemieux says, summarizing his career. "The main objective at the beginning of my career was to win a Stanley Cup. I feel fortunate over the years that I had a chance to win it twice. That was my only goal when I started, to be recognized as a winner and somebody who took a team that was last and brought a winning tradition to Pittsburgh. I think then I can go out in peace.

"I really cherish the days I'm here now and spending time with my kids and my family. That's the important thing to me."

The basement back at 6700 Rue Jogues has changed over the intervening decades since the boys staged their wild hockey nights in Ville Emard. The walls of the largest room of the five-room rowhouse are lined with jerseys and jackets, pictures and portraits, memories of the three brothers Lemieux (mostly Mario). "A shrine," he calls it.

Lemieux has offered to build his parents a palace, but Pierrette didn't want to leave her home of 37 years or her three sisters and their card games. Jean-Guy didn't disagree, but he didn't say much, either. And that tells you a lot about their youngest son.

From his mother Mario inherited his emotional bent, his need for a family circle. From his father he inherited his solitude mistaken for aloofness, his incredible will. For when Jean-Guy was a young boy growing up on a farm far outside Montreal, he too battled sickness — lung problems that kept him off fields of play and under doctors' care.

Their home at 6700 Rue Jogues has changed. The hallway carpet upon which the boys skated was removed for hardwood floor. The 10-by-10 bedroom where the three boys slept was opened to make a roomier kitchen. The basement's tile floor and ceiling have been revamped, and Mario bought the Montreal Forum seats from when Jean-Guy and Pierrette were season-ticket holders.

Yet from the jerseys and the portraits and the photographs and the memories, the basement legend endures.

Maybe the Hockey Hall of Fame should claim the space. For it was a cellar that gave rise to vintage hockey moments, to championships. Fans would gladly pay to enter and raise two Cups to *Le Magnifique.*

Just be mindful of the ceiling.

CHAPTER 2

The Champion

From Worst To First

1984-85	1985-86	1986-87	1987-88
24-51-5	**34-38-8**	**30-38-12**	**36-35-9**
LAST PLACE	5TH PLACE	5TH PLACE	LAST PLACE

BY DAVE MOLINARI
Pittsburgh Post-Gazette

IT WAS THE SPRING OF 1991, AND already Mario Lemieux had three NHL scoring championships, and enough individual trophies and awards to clutter three mantles and a couple of closets. ¶ Hard to imagine a guy cramming more into the first seven seasons of an NHL career, with one pronounced, painful exception: Despite being in the NHL since 1984, Lemieux had less playoff experience than a lot of guys pick up during their first year. ¶ And his exasperation was compounded by fears that a frustrating situation might only get worse, that he would never have a true opportunity to perform on the postseason stage, where sports legends are forged. ¶ Lemieux admitted as much while reflecting on the highs and lows of his career. "After six or seven years of not getting into the playoffs, it was taking its toll," he said.

OK, so maybe his math was off a bit. The Penguins actually failed to qualify for the playoffs in his first few seasons, then slipped into the postseason in 1989. They had a fairly decent run — sweeping the New York Rangers in the first round before losing to Philadelphia in seven games. Lemieux sculpted one of the finest individual performances of his career, scorching the Flyers for five goals and eight points in Game 5.

But the Penguins fizzled in the last two games against Philadelphia, then missed the playoffs in the spring of 1990, in large part because a herniated disk in his back forced Lemieux to sit out 21 of Pittsburgh's final 22 games. They still nearly slipped into the field of 16, only to be eliminated when Buffalo defenseman Uwe Krupp beat goalie Tom Barrasso with a long shot in overtime of the last regular-season game.

The Penguins had needed only a tie against the Sabres to lock up a playoff spot. Lemieux — who flew in a day before the game from Los Angeles, where he had been undergoing therapy on his back since leaving the lineup about six weeks earlier — performed brilliantly in an attempt to make that happen. He scored one goal and assisted on the other, but Krupp's goal negated it all and gave Buffalo a 3-2 victory.

That assured the Penguins of another long summer, and it proved to

be a particularly difficult one for Lemieux. He underwent surgery to remove a portion of his herniated disk in July, and subsequently developed a back infection that forced him to miss the first 50 games of the 1990-91 regular season.

It was, to that point, the nadir of his career, and by the time Lemieux returned to the lineup for a game in Quebec in January 1991, it was obvious he wouldn't have time to put up a typically gaudy point total, let alone make a real run at another Art Ross as the league's top point producer.

Success is not measured solely by statistics, however, and before the 1990-91 season was over, Lemieux had helped to assure it would rank among the most memorable in Penguins history.

Two months after that game in Quebec, the Penguins claimed their first-ever division title. And less than two months later, they were guzzling champagne from the Stanley Cup for the first time. And no one left more fingerprints on the championship that trophy represented than Lemieux.

But while Lemieux captivated the hockey world with some of his work during the championship series against Minnesota, he did not look like a guy destined to do great things when the playoffs began.

Oh, he scored the Penguins' only goal in their playoff opener against New Jersey, a 3-1 defeat at the Civic Arena, but he looked sluggish for much of the series against the Devils. Lemieux later blamed that on medication he was taking for his back, although he made no mention of it at the time.

"I had no energy," he said. "I was weak. I'd go out for warmups and come back and lay down because I had no energy."

1988-89

40-33-7

2ND PLACE,
2ND ROUND
OF PLAYOFFS

1989-90

32-40-8

5TH PLACE

1990-91

41-33-6

STANLEY CUP CHAMPS

1991-92

39-32-9

STANLEY CUP CHAMPS

Nonetheless, the Penguins survived the first round in seven games, thanks in large part to virtuoso performances by low-profile players such as Jiri Hrdina and Frank Pietrangelo. Indeed, back spasms forced Lemieux to sit out the final two periods of the deciding game against New Jersey, which ended in a 4-0 Penguins victory.

Washington offered only token resistance during the second round, which Pittsburgh wrapped up in five games. Again, Lemieux was not a dominant force, but he clearly was beginning to believe that maybe, just maybe, the Penguins might be able to make a serious run at the Cup. And he began to ratchet up his intensity and performance level.

"He got better with each series," said winger Mark Recchi, Lemieux's frequent linemate in the early 1990's. "By the time we reached the semis, you could see the fire in his eyes. You could tell he really wanted it."

Lemieux reinforced that point during Game 2 of the Wales Conference final at Boston Garden. He had two goals and an assist in the Bruins' 5-4 overtime victory, and got the attention of the fellows in the other dressing room. "Their big guy did some pretty good damage," Boston coach Mike Milbury said.

It was, however, another of the Penguins' big guys, left winger Kevin Stevens, who found himself in the spotlight after Game 2. Stevens boldly and repeatedly guaranteed the Penguins would overcome their 2-0 deficit and win the series, a prediction that secured his place in franchise lore.

What isn't so widely known is that even as the sting of the Penguins' Game 2 defeat was sinking in, Penguins center Bryan Trottier was predicting that Lemieux would be responsible for inspiring his team to turn the series around.

"He's shown the boys the way,"

The Penguins had never won a Stanley Cup before Lemieux came along, and under his leadership the team won two in a row.

Lemieux hugs Jaromir Jagr after scoring in Game 4 of the 1992 Stanley Cup finals.

Trottier said. "When the boys see the big boys going ... I can remember with the (New York Islanders), when Clark Gillies stood up in the room or Bobby Nystrom stood up and said, 'Let's go, boys,' we went out on the ice and did it."

Trottier proved prophetic, as Lemieux set up one goal and scored another in the Penguins' 4-1 victory in Game 3, and picked up another goal and assist when Pittsburgh duplicated that score in Game 4. And Lemieux, it turned out, was just getting loose, even though Boston tough guy Chris Nilan had given him a wicked slash across the right wrist late in Game 4.

The series shifted back to Boston for Game 5, and Don Sweeney staked Boston to a 1-0 lead 40 seconds into the game. But Stevens countered that, and Lemieux put the Penguins ahead to stay at 12:04. Before the Penguins' 7-2 victory would become official, Lemieux set up goals by Stevens, Larry Murphy and Ulf Samuelsson.

The Bruins are one of hockey's most proud franchises, and showed their resolve by taking a 2-0 lead midway through the second period of Game 6 at the Civic Arena. Very admirable. But it was the last anyone saw of the Bruins that spring. Murphy, off an assist from Lemieux, got the Penguins jump-started at 11:45 of the second to ignite a three-goal run. Sweeney put Boston even briefly in the third period, but Recchi got the series-winner at 15:40 and Lemieux punctuated the victory with an empty-net goal at 19:32.

That victory hoisted the Penguins into the Stanley Cup finals for the first time, and years later, Lemieux still appreciated what it meant to him to get by the Bruins. "That was the ultimate dream for me when I started, to have a chance to play in the finals," he said.

Lemieux was relatively quiet in Game 1 of the Cup finals against Minnesota, scoring Pittsburgh's second goal in a 5-4 loss at the Civic Arena, but lifted his game to a place where few mortals go for a few rarified seconds during Game 2.

The Penguins were protecting a 2-1 lead late in the second period when Lemieux got the puck in his own zone from Phil Bourque and carried it through the heart of center ice while closing in on Minnesota defensemen Shawn Chambers and Neil Wilkinson.

Lemieux pulled the puck around Chambers, then sliced between him and Wilkinson before faking goalie Jon Casey off his feet and flipping a backhander into the net as he was falling to the ice.

Years later, Penguins center Ron Francis would shake his head at the memory of Lemieux's dazzling show of speed and skill. "By the time he was finished, people in the first 10 rows were lying on their backs, too," Francis said.

IF LEMIEUX WAS TERRIBLY IMpressed by that goal, Pittsburgh's third in a 4-1 victory, he didn't let on. "That's why they pay me a lot," he said at the time.

In the waning days of his career, however, Lemieux said, "I think that was the (goal) I remember the most."

That goal confirmed the North Stars' worst fear: That Lemieux, when healthy and motivated, was almost impossible to stop by legal means.

Oh, the Stars tried their share of illegal tactics to contain him — any team that didn't routinely hook, hold and trip Lemieux when he was in his prime was just daring him to score in double-figures — but it was Lemieux's back that finally neutralized him. Briefly.

Lemieux bent over to untie his skates after going through warmups for Game 3 at the Met Center in Bloomington, Minn. ... and couldn't straighten up. "He said it just locked up on him," Trottier said. "When that happens, it's no go."

And so Lemieux was a last-minute scratch from the Penguins' lineup, and the North Stars reacted to word that he wouldn't play as if they had just won the lottery en masse. "It was like Christmas morning," Minnesota left winger Stewart Gavin said.

The Penguins battled admirably before losing, 3-1. Without hockey's most lethal offensive player, however, they just didn't have enough scoring to manufacture a victory.

"We played a great game, even though we lost," Pittsburgh coach Bob Johnson said. "But if we had had Mario, there's no doubt we would have won."

Charles Burke, the Penguins' team physician, said the back spasms that bothered Lemieux before Game 3 were the same that sidelined him for most of Game 7 against New Jersey. That was why Burke was optimistic Lemieux did not have a long-term problem.

"He got better very quickly before," Burke said. "So he expects to get better very quickly again."

Still, Lemieux's health was the subject of much debate and suspense before Game 4. Edmonton GM Glen Sather, whose playing career included a stint with the Penguins, was asked if he ever had experienced back problems like those of Lemieux. "No," Sather said, "but I've never had to carry a franchise on it, either."

Well, Lemieux was back at work for Game 4, and scored just 22 seconds into his first shift. Because Stevens and Francis had beaten Casey before Lemieux ever stepped onto the ice, his goal gave the Penguins a 3-0 lead in what developed into a 5-3 victory.

Lemieux all but formally wrapped up the Conn Smythe Trophy as playoff MVP during the first period of Game 5, scoring a goal at 5:36 and assisting on two others as the Penguins built a 4-0 lead before holding on for a 6-4 victory.

> *"YOU DREAM OF THIS, BUT IT'S EVEN BETTER IN REAL LIFE THAN IT IS IN YOUR DREAMS."*

Lemieux scored a spectacular shorthanded goal to give the Penguins a 2-0 advantage in the first period of Game 6 and went on to set up goals by Bob Errey, Jim Paek and Larry Murphy. He probably didn't have to bother, though, because the Penguins never were threatened in their 8-0, Cup-clinching victory.

That championship triumph was celebrated in Pittsburgh for days, and left an indelible mark on each of the men who helped to win it. And it was especially significant for Lemieux, who had heard for years that leading a team to the Stanley Cup was the ultimate show of greatness in the NHL.

"To be part of a championship team means everything to me," Lemieux said. "You dream of this, but it's even better in real life than it is in your dreams."

Lemieux's rampage in Game 6

During a victory party at Three Rivers Stadium in 1992, Lemieux shows fans the Stanley Cup.

raised his playoff totals to 16 goals and 28 assists, including five goals and seven assists against Minnesota. Those 44 points were the second-highest total in playoff history, surpassed only by the 47 Wayne Gretzky accumulated during Edmonton's drive to the Cup in 1985.

"Lemieux had a chance to show what he can really do," Johnson said.

"He's an absolutely awesome talent," said Francis, who had joined the Penguins in a trade with Hartford less than three months earlier. "He does some things that are just incredible. And he wanted this so bad, you could see it in his eyes."

And when Lemieux's career was winding down, you could see it in his eyes again. The way they all but misted over as he singled out that championship as the pinnacle of his career.

"Just lifting the Cup the first time we won it (was the highlight)," Lemieux said. "That had been an especially tough year, because I went back surgery and the back infection. I was in bed for three months. I didn't know if I was going to play again."

During the 1991-92 regular season, the Penguins struggled to adjust to the autocratic style of their new coach, Scotty Bowman, who had taken over after Johnson died of brain cancer. Pittsburgh finished third in the Patrick Division with a lackluster 39-32-9 record, and was pitted against Washington, which had the NHL's second-best record in the first round of the playoffs.

THINGS TOOK AN OMINOUS turn for the Penguins in the waning days of the regular season when Lemieux injured his shoulder in a game against New Jersey. That forced him to sit out Game 1, a 3-1 Washington victory.

Lemieux returned to set up power-play goals by Stevens and Murphy in the first 7:07 of Game 2, but Washington ran off six unanswered goals to seize a 2-0 advantage in the series.

In Game 3, Lemieux assisted on the Penguins' first three goals and scored their final three in a 6-4 victory. "It's ridiculous, some of the things he can do," Stevens said.

Nonetheless, Washington embarrassed the Penguins, 7-2, in Game 4 at the Civic Arena, and the Penguins' championship reign appeared to be in its final hours. But at Lemieux's behest, Pittsburgh adopted a conservative style that employed just one forechecking forward, and pulled out a 5-2 victory in Game 5 at the Capital Centre. They were alive.

In Game 6, Lemieux scored two goals and set up three others during a 6-4 victory. That evened the series and staggered the Capitals. "We're lucky to have him here," Stevens said, "so we don't have to try to stop him."

The series went back to Landover for Game 7, and Lemieux keyed the Penguins' 3-1 triumph by scoring a shorthanded goal. Despite sitting out Game 1 with his bad shoulder, he had run up 17 points against Washington, two shy of the NHL record for a single series.

"He took over," Pittsburgh winger Jaromir Jagr said. "That was something I'll never forget."

"We were beaten by just one guy," Capitals coach Terry Murray said. "Lemieux was just too good."

That was hard to argue, but Lemieux never got the chance to be much of a factor during the second round against the Rangers. At 5:05 of the first period in Game 2, Adam Graves broke a bone in Lemieux's left hand with a baseball-style slash.

That meant Lemieux could only watch as the Penguins, led by a remarkable effort from Francis, rallied to defeat New York in six games. Still, there was no assurance Lemieux would be back in uniform before Pittsburgh's playoff run ended. Doctors had predicted that his fracture would need 4-6 weeks to heal, and that he would have difficulty gripping a stick for 3-4 weeks.

No one was surprised, then, when he didn't dress for Game 1 of the Wales Conference final against Boston, a 4-3 Pittsburgh victory in overtime, but Lemieux decided on the morning of Game 2 that he was ready to return. For light duty. Maybe just a little power-play time.

Nice idea, but before evening ended, Lemieux was playing on the power-play and penalty-killing units, as well as taking a regular shift. And, oh yeah, recording two goals and an assist in Pittsburgh's 5-2 victory.

"Whatever effect any other player has on his team when he returns from an injury, Mario does it tenfold," Trottier said.

FIVE YEARS LATER, FRANCIS still marveled at how quickly Lemieux had been able to rejoin the lineup, and at the impact he had upon returning.

"When he broke his hand in the Rangers series, I figured he was pretty much done for a while," Francis said. "I was surprised to see him back as quick as he was against the Bruins. Not only back, but playing as well as he did the rest of the way. If he didn't come back, we probably wouldn't have accomplished what we did."

The Penguins clinched the series with a couple of victories at Boston Garden, but it was a goal Lemieux scored during Game 4 that will be the enduring memory from that conference final.

Pittsburgh was killing a holding penalty to defenseman Paul Stanton when Lemieux carried the puck through center ice. As Ray Bourque, Boston's All-World defenseman, was frantically skating to stay ahead of him, Lemieux pushed the puck be-

At the White House, President George Bush congratulates Lemieux and the Penguins on their championship season in 1991.

tween Bourque's legs. He then picked it up on the other side before charging to the net and whipping a shot over goalie Andy Moog's glove.

"I told him that when I write my book, that one gets a chapter," Francis said.

That goal, like the one he scored in Game 2 against Minnesota in 1991, was so extraordinary that the passage of time took away none of its luster.

"He absolutely blew by Ray Bourque, and four or five years ago, Ray Bourque was still in his prime," Peter Taglianetti said. "Things like that, you just gawk at."

Beating Boston got the Penguins a spot in the Cup final for the second year in a row, but Pittsburgh didn't look like it belonged there early in Game 1. The Blackhawks built a 4-1 lead before the Penguins began to compete with them.

Once Pittsburgh's comeback got rolling, however, there was no stopping it. And, predictably, Lemieux was the guy out in front.

The Penguins were down, 4-2, late in the second period when Lemieux scored that kind of goal that would be dumb luck for most players, but was sheer talent for him. He had the puck behind the Chicago goal line and, with no direct route to the inside of the net, opted to bank it in off the leg of Blackhawks goalie Ed Belfour. The same way he victimized numerous other goalies with impossible-angle shots throughout his career.

Lemieux was not finished, however. With the game tied, 4-4, and the Penguins on a power play, Lemieux punched a Larry Murphy rebound into the net with 12.6 seconds left in regulation for the 5-4 Penguins victory.

Only two teams have won a Cup final game after trailing, 4-1 — Montreal in 1944 and Pittsburgh in 1992.

"Before every game, you'd wonder what you were going to see," Murphy said of Lemieux. "The years we won the Cups, the thing you noticed was what impact he had on opposing goalies. They'd come into the finals riding a pretty good wave, feeling pretty good about themselves, and it would take him a game, a game-and-a-half, to really strike some doubt into their minds."

Not everyone held Lemieux in such high esteem. Between Games 1 and 2, Chicago coach Mike Keenan accused Lemieux of diving to draw the hooking penalty that led to his game-winning goal. Lemieux Keenan said, was "an embarrassment to himself, to the game and to the players he's playing with."

Keenan was looking for a psychological edge, but Lemieux wouldn't be rattled. "No comment," Lemieux said, "at this point."

Lemieux picked up his fifth game-winning goal of the playoffs in Pittsburgh's 3-1 victory in Game 2, tying the NHL record shared by Mike Bossy, Jari Kurri and Bobby Smith, and the Penguins pushed the Blackhawks to the brink of elimination with a 1-0 victory in Game 3 at Chicago Stadium.

LEMIEUX THEN SCORED THE Penguins' third goal in their Cup-clinching, 6-5 victory in Game 4, and joined Bernie Parent of Philadelphia as the only players to earn the Conn Smythe Trophy in back-to-back years. Never mind that his shoulder and hand injuries had prevented Lemieux from even dressing for six of Pittsburgh's 21 playoff games.

Mind you, his playoff stats — 16 goals and 18 assists in 15 games — were none too shabby. Neither was his sense of humor, as evidenced by the jab he aimed at Keenan while speaking to reporters after Game 4.

"I'm just going to go in the locker room and try to dive in the Cup now," Lemieux said.

Winning the Cup for the second time inspired the Penguins to talk about a burgeoning dynasty, but it was not to be. They had an extraordinary team in 1992-93, winning the President's Trophy by compiling the league's best regular-season record, but were upset in the second round of the playoffs by the Islanders.

The Pittsburgh teams of the early 1990's might be remembered as much for what they might have accomplished as for what they actually accomplished.

"Ninety-two was a great team, but I think '93 was a better team, stronger," Lemieux said. "We just couldn't get the job done. For four years, I played on a great team. It was a lot of fun to play every night because we were so strong, dominating games. You really cherish those times."

But he never forgot the ones that preceded those heady days, either. Lemieux, you see, wasn't simply the driving force behind the Penguins' Stanley Cups. He was the guy who kept hockey alive in Pittsburgh, and made it possible for interest in the game to flourish.

The franchise was on life-support before the Penguins claimed Lemieux with the first choice in the 1984 Entry Draft. Attendance rarely rose above four figures during the 1983-84 season, when Pittsburgh finished with a league-low 38 points, and the most wildly optimistic assessment of the team was that it faced an uncertain future. "It was very tenuous, at best," said Terry Schiffhauer, the Penguins' public-relations director in those days.

THE YEAR BEFORE LEMIEUX arrived, the Penguins claimed an average attendance of 6,838. Too bad they couldn't inflate their victories total the way they did crowd sizes. "I would say we never padded it by more than 600 in a game," Schiffhauer said, smiling.

Didn't matter. The Civic Arena was empty, cold and lifeless on most game nights, and perhaps that was fitting. The franchise looked to be on its deathbed, with the only possible cure being a new home. Several cities showed interest and, while it isn't certain how close former owner Edward DeBartolo came to moving and/or selling the club, the threat of having the Penguins leave town was legitimate.

"You always hated to pick up the papers and see that Phoenix was interested, or Hamilton," Schiffhauer said.

Reviving such a moribund operation would not be easy. Pittsburgh had little talent at the major-league level, no farm system to speak of and no marquee player to hold the fans' attention while the team went through the long and grueling process of rebuilding.

"It was on very shaky ground," said Eddie Johnston, Pittsburgh's general manager at the time. "We needed an impact player. We were just foundering. We needed a shot in the arm, and the only guy in the draft who I felt was a franchise player was Mario."

Not everyone agreed. Neil Smith, now general manager of the New York Rangers, was a scout for Detroit in 1984 and believed Kirk Muller was the top player available in that draft. Other scouts and team officials agreed.

Johnston did not. He ignored those on his staff who urged him to accept one of the lucrative trade packages being dangled before him by Montreal and Quebec, and never gave up on the notion that Lemieux was the guy who could save the franchise. Rarely has a management decision been so publicly and profoundly vindicated.

"There's no question," Johnston said. "If we didn't take him, (the Civic Arena) would be a parking lot now."

When Lemieux arrived, the mindset of the entire organization began to change. Finally, the future was acknowledged to be something later than next week. No longer were most decisions made with nothing more in mind than their immediate impact, with all long-term consequences ignored.

"It always seemed like we were going hand-to-mouth," Schiffhauer said. "That every year in March the goal was to make a run for the playoffs and give up whatever we had to from

"HOPEFULLY, I'LL BE REM

the future because the playoffs are the answer this year, and we'll worry about next year, next year."

And so Johnston set about trying to construct a sound organization, with Lemieux as his cornerstone. He might not have seemed the perfect candidate for the role — Lemieux was a shy 18-year-old with a limited command of English, his second language — but Lemieux understood that he and the paying public had to be patient, that a weak team could not be transformed to a contender in a matter of weeks or months.

"I knew it was going to take time when I came to Pittsburgh," he said. "I gave myself five years to try to put a good team together. We struggled for a while with the personnel we had, but I was ready to make the commitment and be patient. I'm glad I was part of keeping the team in Pittsburgh."

The fans responded immediately. The Penguins' average attendance increased by about 3,200 during his rookie season. The championships Lemieux craved followed in 1991.

Long before that, however, Lemieux had taken care of the most important facet of his mandate: He had made the Penguins a viable, valuable operation in Pittsburgh. To those who saw the decrepit state of the franchise in the early 1980's, that is perhaps Lemieux's most remarkable accomplishment.

"Sometimes, he probably doesn't get enough credit," said Wayne Gretzky, who set most of the standards by which Lemieux is measured. "Pittsburgh was getting 6,000 people a game when he got there, so he basically saved that franchise and then won two Cups."

Lemieux's legacy will not be limited to the championships the Penguins captured when he was their captain, however. He is the primary reason that rinks have popped up across Western Pennsylvania in recent years. The reason a generation of young players took up the game.

EMBERED AS A *WINNER.*"

When the Penguins drafted Lemieux, there were only a handful of rinks scattered around the region. Lately, it seems that almost every municipality has one, is getting one, or would like to get one.

It's unlikely the boom in Pittsburgh will have such a significant impact on the NHL, but it's perfectly reasonable to believe the caliber and quantity of young players coming out of the Pittsburgh area will continue to rise for years.

"When I first got here (in 1990), there were only two or three rinks where kids could skate," Taglianetti said. "All of a sudden, these dual rinks are popping up all over the place. It's just amazing.

"There's going to be a big (talent) pool here for a lot of Division I colleges to come look at because of Mario."

Lemieux's breathtaking talents are what captivated Pittsburgh, of course, but the off-ice ties he developed to the city didn't go unnoticed. At a time when even the most prominent players switch teams with alarming regularity, Lemieux never has drawn a paycheck from anyone except the Penguins.

"That's something I'm very proud of, that I had the opportunity to play for one team throughout my career," he said.

Mind you, he made millions of dollars doing it, but the Penguins and their fans got a pretty hefty payback for all they gave Lemieux. If they're not satisfied, they should be. Lemieux certainly is.

"I played for 12 years, and I feel pretty comfortable having won two Cups, the (two) Conn Smythes and with what I've accomplished throughout my career," he said.

"I just want to be remembered as somebody who was able to take a team that was the worst in the league and was able to bring a championship to Pittsburgh. I'm very proud that I accomplished that.

"And, hopefully, I'll be remembered as a winner."

CHAPTER 3

The Legacy

Leaving His Mark

By Ron Cook
Pittsburgh Post-Gazette

IT WASN'T SUPPOSED to end like this. A 6-3 loss to the Philadelphia Flyers in the first round of the 1997 Stanley Cup playoffs? ¶ Mario Lemieux was supposed to go out a winner. He was supposed to end his spectacular career with the Pittsburgh Penguins by hoisting the Stanley Cup one final time. He came close in 1996. The Penguins lost to the Florida Panthers on home ice in Game 7 of the Eastern Conference finals. He really liked their chances in 1997. ¶ Another Cup would have made The Lemieux Story too much of a fairy tale. ¶ His life has been anything but. ¶ That might be hard for people who aren't familiar with the intimate details of his career to understand. The Penguins won the Cup in 1991 and 1992, didn't they? He won the Conn Smythe Trophy as playoff MVP in both years. He won the Hart Trophy three times as NHL MVP and the Art Ross Trophy six times as the league's leading scorer. He retired as the most consistent goal-scorer in NHL history, averaging .823 per game, and trailed only Wayne Gretzky in points (2.005) and assists (1.18) per game. He finished in sixth place on the NHL's all-time goals list (613), 11th in assists (881) and sixth in points (1,494). His adoring fans in Pittsburgh will tell you he's clearly the greatest player ever, although Gretzky loyalists will argue the point.

But there also have been many dark moments along the way. His back surgeries in 1990 and 1993. His successful battle against cancer in 1993. The 275 regular-season games he missed because of injury or illness.

"He might have had 900 goals," former Penguins coach Eddie Johnston once gushed.

"If I would have played more games and been healthy my whole career, maybe I would be up there with Gretzky," Lemieux said. "We'll never know, I guess."

Not that Lemieux has any regrets. "Not at all. Thirteen years is a long time to play. I've done a lot, winning the two Cups. ... I wanted to leave the game close to being at the top of my game. I've been able to do that. I'm very satisfied with my career."

It's almost impossible to pick out Lemieux's greatest moment. He cherishes the two Cup years as well as his 199-point season in 1988-89, the fifth-best point total in NHL history. That was the year, in an 8-6 victory against the New Jersey Devils Dec. 31, that he became the only player to score five different kinds of goals in the same

Lemieux follows Jaromir Jagr onto the Civic Arena ice for a 1997 playoff game against the Philadelphia Flyers.

OUCH!

LEMIEUX'S BAD BACK MADE HIM A TARGET FOR CHEAP SHOTS

game — even strength, short-handed, on a power play, on a penalty shot and into an empty net. "By far, that was my best year," Lemieux said.

BUT AN EVEN GREATER MEASURE of his wondrous skills might be what he did in his final two seasons after sitting out 1994-95 because of health problems. Among other things, he:

◆ Won his third Hart Trophy in 1996 and his final two Ross trophies in 1996 and 1997.

◆ Scored a career-high five goals in an 8-4 victory against the Gretzky-led St. Louis Blues March 26, 1996, two days after his third child, Austin Nicholas, was born three months premature.

◆ Had a seven-game goal-scoring streak in the 1996 playoffs before being held to one goal in seven games by Florida's suffocating defense.

◆ Had two goals and an assist in the 1997 All-Star Game in San Jose Jan. 18, tying Gretzky for most career All-Star points with 20. Afterward, he joked about his next appearance during All-Star weekend — in the Heroes of Hockey game for the old-timers. "I'll be a rookie."

◆ Scored four goals in the third period of a 5-2 victory at Montreal Jan. 26, 1997, thrilling fans who had watched him as boy growing up in the city. "He just came and showed that he's the man," Penguins goaltender Patrick Lalime marveled.

◆ Scored his 600th goal in a 6-4 victory against Vancouver Feb. 4, 1997, before a delirious crowd at Pittsburgh's Civic Arena. "Having it happen here in front of these fans is something I'll remember for a while," Lemieux said.

◆ Had two goals and three assists in an 8-5 loss to Montreal March 26, 1997, in his final appearance before the Canadiens fans, who gave him a thunderous ovation when he was named the game's No. 1 star. "That's tear-jerking," Penguins general manager/coach Craig Patrick said. "The fans were fabulous. Mario deserves it."

◆ Performed magic on the same line with teammates Jaromir Jagr and Ron Francis during the 1996-97 season. "Superman, Batman and Robin," New York Islanders center Travis Green called them.

A lot of people feared Superman hung up his cape for good after the 1993-94 season. Everybody knew of Lemieux's fight with Hodgkin's disease, how he took his final radiation treatment on the morning of March 2, 1993, then played against the Flyers that night, getting a goal and an assist in a 5-4 loss.

What they didn't know was how the treatments and the dozens of cortisone shots he took for his back over the years robbed Lemieux of his strength, not just during the rest of the 1993 season, but in the next season as well. He was fatigued constantly.

Lemieux's back also continued to ache. He had his second surgery July 28, 1993. He played in only 22 games in 1993-94. "There were many nights we literally picked him up off the training table and propelled him into the locker room," said Dr. Chip Burke, the Penguins' orthopedist. "He would be playing at 25 percent. He was still better than anyone else."

That wasn't good enough for Lemieux. He especially wasn't happy with his performance in the Penguins' loss to the Washington Capitals in the first round of the 1994 playoffs.

"This wasn't a close call," Lemieux's agent, Tom Reich, said Aug. 29, 1994, the day Lemieux announced he was taking a one-year medical sabbatical from hockey.

"I still love the game," Lemieux said at the time. "This is not a hockey issue. It's a health issue. Hopefully, the fans will understand my health is more important than hockey. If they don't, I think they have a problem."

Lemieux talked of making a comeback. "There's a strong possibility I will be able to come back. It's just a matter of regaining my strength and working on my back for a year."

Still, it was easy for everyone, including teammates, to have doubts.

Time flies: Lemieux and Gretzky were Canada Cup teammates in 1987, opponents a decade later.

Would Lemieux have the same commitment to hockey after a season off? Would he have the discipline to leave the golf course to rehabilitate his back? And, maybe most troubling, if he came back, would he be able to accept, heaven forbid, being something less than the greatest player in the world?

"That was the hardest part for me," said NFL Hall of Famer Paul Hornung. He missed the 1963 season because of a one-year gambling suspension before resuming his career with the Green Bay Packers.

"No great player is happy with anything less than his best. I know I hated it when I came back and I couldn't kick like I used to. About one out of every four kicks, my leg wouldn't lock. I remember once I kicked an extra point into the left guard's butt. Fuzzy Thurston turned around and said, 'What the hell are you doing, Hornung? Betting again?'

"I hated that failure."

Lemieux had the same worries.

He admitted he liked his new lifestyle. He enjoyed spending time with his wife, Nathalie, and, at that time, his one daughter, Lauren. And he loved his golf, maybe his greatest passion.

EVENTUALLY, THOUGH, HOCKEY brought Lemieux back. He traveled with the Penguins during the 1995 playoffs and watched them come back from a three-games-to-one deficit in the first round to beat the Capitals before losing to the eventual Stanley Cup champion Devils in the second round. He thought about just how good the Penguins

JOFA
C
66

U.S.
OLEST
C
66
66
JOFA
KOHO
REVOLUTION
KOHO

would be if he played again.

The announcement that all of Pittsburgh was eager to hear came June 20, 1995. "I'm going to play again," Lemieux said. Actually, the entire hockey world, with the possible exception of the goaltenders, was eager to hear that news.

"Mario is too good a player to be playing golf," Philadelphia winger Kevin Dineen said. "There are a lot of good golfers out there, but there's only one guy who plays hockey the way he does. Nobody can do it. I've seen Eric Lindros try to play that style and he can't do it. Gretzky doesn't have the reach Mario has. He's just so talented and skilled with the puck, he makes guys around him so much better."

Lemieux said even he was a bit surprised by his decision to play again. "This time last year, I thought my career was over and I had no plans of coming back. But in the last six months, I started feeling stronger, I was not as fatigued and my back was much better. During the last few months, I started to think I could play this game again."

Then, in a statement that must have chilled those NHL goaltenders, Lemieux added, "I'm not coming back to be an average player. I want to come back and be one of the top players in the world. If I can get back in decent shape, I think I can get my game to where it was a couple of years ago."

It seemed like such a huge "if."

LEMIEUX WAS NEVER KNOWN for his off-season conditioning. He never had to train. The game just came so easily to him. "He's a different player than anybody else," Jagr said. "He's like a Michael Jordan. It's natural. He was born with it. He does-

Lemieux baffled NHL goalies year after year with his remarkable skill and athletic ability.

Lemieux weds longtime girlfriend Nathalie Asselin in Montreal in June 1993. One reason he retired early was to spend more time with his family.

n't have to do much. He doesn't have to work out, lift weights. His upper body is still going to be the strongest. That's a gift. No one else has it. That's why he's so good."

Francis tells of a wonderful conversation he had with Lemieux in the summer of 1991, not long after the Penguins had won their first Cup. They had just finished a round of golf and were sipping beers at the 19th hole. "Mario, do you ever work out in the summer?"

"Yeah."

"You do? What do you do?"

"Starting Aug. 1, I don't order any French fries with my club sandwich."

Lemieux laughs when he is reminded of this, but he doesn't dispute the story. "My skill level was so high that I didn't need to train when I was 18, 20, 21 years old. I just used to come to training camp and get in shape in two weeks and I was at the top of my game."

Give Lemieux credit for realizing those days were gone forever. He was going to turn 30 two days before the start of his comeback season. He knew what he had to do. He installed a gym in his home and began working out for 90 minutes a day, stretching, riding a bike, walking a treadmill and lifting weights. He hired Tom Plasko, a massage therapist, to supervise his workouts.

"He's doing tremendous," Plasko said on the day Lemieux announced his comeback. "His shoulder size has increased. His arms have increased. We want to put on bulk without adding weight."

Lemieux's coaches and teammates were pleasantly surprised a few months later when he showed up for the start of training camp.

"This is the best shape I've ever seen him in," said Gilles Meloche, the Penguins' goaltending coach and one of Lemieux's closest friends.

The night of Oct. 7, 1995, couldn't come quickly enough for Penguins fans. That was the night of the season opener against Toronto. It was as if Lemieux had never been gone. He didn't beat goaltender Felix Potvin that night, but he did have four assists in the Penguins' 8-3 victory. The sellout crowd at the Civic Arena knew they were watching something special. Lemieux was given several loud, long standing ovations.

"Yeah, I had my doubts (about coming back)," Lemieux said after the game. "I was really nervous the past couple of days. I didn't know how to approach this game. I've had quite a few comebacks here, but it's always nice to hear that ovation from the crowd."

That night was the start of a fascinating season. Just about everyone who watched it unfold gave Lemieux rave reviews. He played in 70 regular-season games, about 10 more than he had planned. His 69 goals, 92 assists and 161 points led the league.

"For a guy who was out almost a year and a half, it's amazing what he did," Johnston said. "Let's face it, if he would have played all the games, he might have gotten 200 points."

Lemieux was especially brilliant through most of the 1996 playoffs. He had eight goals in five games as the Penguins blew away the New York Rangers in the second round. Jagr had five goals in the series.

"You have to go back to Bobby Orr and Phil Esposito to find two guys on the same team like Mario and Jags," Johnston said. "I played with those guys in Boston. Now, I have Lemieux and Jagr here. I've been blessed."

Johnston wouldn't say which pairing was better. He and Orr remain

"I WANT
TO SPEND
MORE
TIME
WITH MY
WIFE.
I WANT
TO SEE
MY
THREE
KIDS
GROW UP.
I WANT
TO PLAY
GOLF IN
FLORIDA
DURING
THE
WINTERS."

The big three in the Steel City: linemates Jaromir Jagr, Ron Francis and Mario Lemieux.

close friends. And he wouldn't say anything to even slightly offend Lemieux and Jagr.

But you might be surprised who was willing to pick a pair.

"We couldn't score the way those guys are scoring," Orr said. "Holy heck, we weren't that good.

"That Jagr kid is a real force. And Lemieux is the most talented player I've ever seen. This guy is unbelievable, not just offensively but defensively. I'm watching him in his own end and I'm thinking, 'Holy mackerel, who is that guy?' He's the best defensive player on the ice."

THAT WAS ESPECIALLY TRUE in that series against the Rangers. They went a miserable 4 for 23 on the power play. Wouldn't you know that Lemieux was the Penguins' chief penalty killer? No player has ever had his size, reach, quickness and instincts in the defensive zone.

"He's so good at reading the play," Johnston said. "He puts himself in the right position so that the other team always has to make a pass through him."

Lemieux failed to satisfy only one critic with his play in 1995-96. "It was not a good year for me," he said.

There was another bout with fatigue at midseason. "I'm tired all the time," Lemieux said. "No energy at all, to the point where I can't work out the way I used to. It shows in my performance on the ice."

There was never an explanation for his problems after doctors ruled out a thyroid condition.

There also was the worry that went with finding another lump on his neck. Thankfully, that turned out to be a false alarm.

And there was the anguish that went with his wife's troublesome pregnancy with their son. "It's been very difficult for myself and my family the last couple of months," Lemieux said after his breakout, five-goal game against St. Louis.

"By the way I was playing, I think everybody knew something was up. I was not able to play very well. I think my head was somewhere else."

Despite those problems, Lemieux still averaged better than two points a game — 2.3, to be exact — a feat only he and Gretzky have accomplished. One more goal would have given him an even 70. That's one goal a game, for you math majors.

"I had a lot of points, but it was frustrating," Lemieux said. "I couldn't do the things I used to do.

"Not even close. I had lost a step or two. I struggled with the fact I couldn't beat people one-on-one like I used to."

For a long time it looked as if Lemieux was going to quit after that 1996 season. He was angry with NHL officials for continuing to allow lesser players to clutch and grab the stars, thereby limiting their effectiveness. He was especially angry with himself after his play against Florida in the confer-

ence finals. Statistically, it was his worst playoff series. He was so frustrated that late in Game 7, just as the sand was starting to pour out of the Penguins' hour glass, he found himself in a scrum with Brian Skrudland, losing two minutes to an unnecessary penalty call. Those who watched that night wondered if their last impression of No. 66 would be him shaking hands with that noted brick wall, Panthers goaltender John Vanbiesbrouck.

Lemieux offered no clues about his future throughout the 1996 summer. Even in June, when he attended the NHL awards dinner in Toronto to pick up his Hart and Ross trophies, he was vague, saying the Penguins' ability to upgrade their personnel in the coming weeks "would make a big difference" in his decision to play another year or retire.

"If the team wants to go in a direction where they want to have another shot at the Cup, I'd love to be part of it. If not, I would weigh that."

The Sergei Zubov-for-Kevin Hatcher trade with Dallas helped Lemieux make up his mind. "With the changes we made over the summer, I think we're definitely going in the right direction. Hatcher is somebody I respect a lot. I always find it tough to play against him. That was one element on our team that was missing last year."

A meeting in New York with NHL Commissioner Gary Bettman and Director of Hockey Operations Brian Burke also influenced Lemieux's decision. They told him the league was going to crack down on the obstruction fouls Lemieux despises. "They want to improve the game by opening it up and making it more fun for the players and the fans. Hopefully, it's going to last more than a couple of weeks."

Lemieux made it official Sept. 9, 1996. "I want to come back and try to win the Cup again. That's my only goal."

Two months into the season, Lemieux thought he had made a terrible decision. The Penguins stumbled to a 6-13-1 start. His numbers in those 20 games — nine goals and 17 assists — would have been superb for most players. He found them abysmal.

Patrick salvaged the Penguins' season. In a three-day span from Nov. 17-19, he traded for defensemen Darius Kasparaitis, Jason Woolley and Fredrik Olausson, and forwards Stu Barnes, Alex Hicks and Andreas Johansson. Beginning Nov. 22, the team went on a 20-2-4 run.

Johnston salvaged Lemieux's season. In the Nov. 22 game at Hartford, he put Lemieux, Jagr and Francis on the same line for the first time. The results were magical.

"The people here, they'll never see anything like this again," Johnston said. "I've been watching hockey all my life and I've never seen a line like this."

The best ever? "I can't name a line any better," Johnston said, shrugging.

LEMIEUX AND FRANCIS ARE locks to make the Hall of Fame. Jagr, who turned 25 during the 1996-97 season, will get there barring a catastrophic injury.

Three Hall of Famers on the same line have happened occasionally. Oldtimers have a hard time deciding which was better — the Kraut Line of Milt Schmidt, Woody Dumart and Bobby Bauer in Boston, the Production Line of Gordie Howe, Ted Lindsay and Sid Abel in Detroit, or the Montreal line of Rocket Richard, Toe Blake and Elmer Lach. Richard's 50 goals in 50 games in 1944-45 remain one of the game's most incredible feats.

More recently, Guy Lafleur, Steve Shutt and Jacques Lemaire played together in Montreal. All made the Hall.

Statistically, Boston's Esposito, Johnny Bucyk (or Ken Hodge) and Wayne Cashman were the NHL's top line. Hall of Famers Esposito and Bucyk, along with Cashman, combined for an astonishing 1,550 goals during their careers, easily the most by any three linemates. Lemieux, Jagr and Francis have a total of 1,282 by comparison.

"I played with those guys in Boston, and these guys are better,"

Lemieux demonstrates his puck-handling skills as he outmaneuvers a pair of defenders during a game against the Hartford Whalers.

Johnston said. "Their speed separates them. All three can finish plays. And their skill level is out of sight."

The Triple Crown Line of Marcel Dionne, Charlie Simmer and Dave Taylor in Los Angeles put up some amazing numbers — the players combined for 1,504 goals during their careers — but the Kings never won anything. Nor did the Buffalo teams that featured the line of Gilbert Perreault, Rene Robert and Rick Martin.

Philadelphia fans will argue for the Flyers' line of Bobby Clarke, Bill Barber and Reggie Leach in the 1970's. Their teams won two Stanley Cups and Clarke and Barber made the Hall. Philly fans also will try to make a case for the Flyers' Legion of Doom line of Lindros, John LeClair and Mikael Renberg.

Sorry, there's just no comparison.

With apologies to Lindros, Lemieux and Jagr were the best two players in the league in 1996-97. No one can remember another line with the two best players of their time. Esposito and Orr don't count because Orr was a defenseman.

Gretzky and Jari Kurri were terrific on the great Edmonton teams, but they played with a revolving left wing. Esa Tikkanen was their best linemate, but, more often than not, it was a tough guy such as Dave Semenko, who was on the ice to protect them.

Bryan Trottier and Mike Bossy were an intriguing pair on the great New York Islanders teams. Trottier was the best two-way player of his generation, is the sport's ninth-leading scorer and will go into the Hall of Fame the instant he's eligible in the fall of 1997. Hall of Famer Bossy was the best pure goal-scorer of his time. They played with Clark Gillies, a good, tough player.

"This line is way better than we were," said Trottier, a Penguins' assistant coach. "That's no slight to Mike and me. We gave 'em fits at times. It's just that Mario and Jaromir can do so many things with the puck. And when you put them with a guy with Ronnie's hands. ... It's absolutely scary."

Lemieux, Jagr and Francis combined for 80 goals and 187 points in the 39 regular-season games they played together.

"It's been a lot of fun," Lemieux said during the team's 14-game unbeaten streak at midseason. "It's nice to know there's a good chance we can make a great play every time we're out there."

Lemieux averaged 1.82 points per game when he played with Jagr and Francis, 1.38 in the 37 games when he did not. He had a 15-game scoring streak end when he missed the Jan. 23 game against Colorado because of back spasms, but he came back three days later to score those four goals at Montreal.

"I've never seen him play better," Trottier said. "I've never seen him take charge like this."

"He has that old jump in his legs again," Johnston said.

Said Lemieux, "I'll never be the same player I once was, but I'm close. In my prime, I always felt like I could change the pace of a game either by slowing it down or speeding it up. I'm doing a little bit of that right now."

Everybody wonders what Lemieux's career might have been if not for his chronic back pain and his cancer. But what would his career have looked like if he had played more with Jagr and Francis? How many more scoring titles and MVP awards would he have won if he hadn't spent so much

carrying the Jock Callanders and Butsy Ericksons of the world? Where would he rank on the career scoring lists if he hadn't played so often with the Wilf Paiements and Brad Aitkens?

"It's unfathomable," Johnston said.

Only once in his career did Lemieux play with linemates even faintly resembling Jagr and Francis. The Lemieux-Kevin Stevens-Rick Tocchet line combined for 172 goals and 380 points in 1992-93, even though Lemieux missed 20 games because of the cancer.

"Those guys were perfect for me," Lemieux said. "Both were big guys who could get open and score goals. They just needed someone to carry the puck."

Part of the Lemieux-Jagr-Francis success is communication.

"He listens when Jaromir or I say something," Francis said. "I think a lot of guys he's played with over the years have been intimidated by him.

"He's a legend. They figure, 'Why should I suggest anything to him? He knows everything.' But we're always talking on the ice."

"The communication between us is great," Lemieux said. "It's nice not to have to dictate everything that happens out there."

It's no coincidence the Penguins sagged after Johnston, then still the Penguins coach, broke up the line in mid-February. He had no choice. Jagr pulled a groin muscle that forced him to miss 16 of 17 games.

The Penguins lost 10 of 11. That was enough to get Johnston fired March 3 and put Patrick behind the bench. At one point, the team went 4-19-2.

Lemieux's game suffered badly.

He went three consecutive games without a point and eight in a row without a goal, the longest such streaks of his career. Francis also struggled. He

Lemieux, who resuscitated the Penguins franchise, will be missed.

LEMIEUX
66
McDonald's
Bud ICE
HAT TRICK!

Lemieux responds to cheers following his final Civic Arena appearance on April 23, 1997.

It didn't help Lemieux and Francis that they had to battle nagging injuries. Lemieux injured his hip when he was jerked to the ice in a game against Calgary on Jan. 21. Francis was troubled by back and groin problems.

"Every time this happens with my back and hip, my legs take a beating," Lemieux said. "I lose my quickness and strength and it takes a long time to get it back."

Patrick did the only thing he could do to jump-start Lemieux, Francis and the Penguins. He reunited the line when Jagr returned March 29 against Los Angeles. The team won that day, 4-1, as the line combined for two goals and five assists.

All was well again — at least temporarily — in the Penguins' world.

Unfortunately for the Penguins, the good times didn't last. Jagr strained his groin again and had to miss the final two regular-season games. The team limped into the playoffs.

Its stay was brief. The Flyers won four of five games, outscored the Penguins, 20-13, outshot them, 213-139, and outhit them from start to finish.

"They just overpowered us, especially their power forwards down low," Lemieux said. "They were just too big and strong for us."

Lemieux was no better than the fourth-best player in the series behind Jagr and the Flyers' Lindros and LeClair. He finished with respectable numbers — three goals and three assists — but was never Lemieux-like at any point in the series unless you count the goal he scored on a breakaway near the end of the Penguins' 4-1 victory in Game 4.

"It was awful for me," Lemieux said of the series. "I didn't have my legs. I didn't have my strength. I just ran out of gas the last month of the season. Not being able to play the way I once did is very frustrating for me. I just can't accept that. That's one of the reasons I'm retiring now."

Although Lemieux, 31, didn't get that third Stanley Cup, he did have the satisfaction of walking away on his terms. How many other athletes have gone out on the top of their game or near it? Joe DiMaggio. Jim Brown. Rocky Marciano. Try to name more.

Lemieux retired also knowing he was the greatest athlete in Pittsburgh sports history. Maybe fans of the great Pirates shortstop, Honus Wagner, would argue if they were alive. Arnold Palmer fans certainly will argue. But nothing was quite as much fun as watching Lemieux perform his art. Not Bill Mazeroski turning a double play, Roberto Clemente making a throw from right field or Barry Bonds hitting a screamer into the gap. Not Terry Bradshaw throwing a bomb to Lynn Swann, Jack Lambert squashing a running back or Jack Ham outthinking every quarterback he lined up against.

"I want to spend more time with my wife. I want to see my kids grow up." A fourth Lemieux child was due in 1997. "I want to play golf in Florida during the winters," he said. "Actually, I'm looking forward to retirement."

To say Lemieux will be missed is a gross understatement.

"He's been the Jean Beliveau of our era," said the Rangers' Mark Messier. "Nobody's played with the pure grace, elegance and power that Mario possesses. He's got a style all his own."

Colin Campbell, who coaches the Rangers, maybe the Penguins' most hated rivals, is like a lot of other NHL coaches and goaltenders. In one sense, he's thrilled he won't have to face Lemieux again. But in another, bigger sense, he's saddened by Lemieux's departure. The game just won't be the same without him.

"I don't know who's going to carry his torch," Campbell said.

It's a heavy torch, indeed.

CHAPTER 4

The Memories

Mario's Magic Moments

RANGERS
KOHO

6-9-84

“*If they satisfy me, I would love to play in Pittsburgh.*”

MARIO LEMIEUX

PENGUINS TO SELECT MARIO LEMIEUX AS THE TOP DRAFT PICK

SAVIOR-IN-WAITING

SEEKS BIG CONTRACT

PLAYING HARDBALL

SUITORS ABOUND

By Bruce Keidan
Pittsburgh Post-Gazette

MONTREAL — LIKE IT OR NOT, Mario Lemieux will become the property of the Penguins this afternoon. Lemieux, who is better at playing center than playing coy, is having a hard time disguising his glee over that fact. ¶ The golden boy of junior hockey, Lemieux will be the first player selected in the National Hockey League entry draft. Contract negotiations between the Penguins and the 18-year-old savior-in-waiting lurched to a halt late last week, but both the player and the team seem to feel that the problem is surmountable. ¶ "I don't want to go back to juniors (hockey)," the 6-foot-4, 200-pound forward confirmed yesterday afternoon. ¶ "If they satisfy me, I would love to play in Pittsburgh. The future is in Pittsburgh." ¶ Lemieux has never been to Pittsburgh, but he has seen "Flashdance," which is close enough. He continued to hold out the

From left, Kirk Muller (No. 2), Lemieux (No. 1) and Ed Olczyk (No. 3) — the NHL's top three draft picks in 1984.

possibility that he might boycott today's draft at the Forum, but admitted that was really nothing more than a negotiating ploy. "They might agree to make me a better offer," he said, "because they'd look pretty stupid if the No. 1 pick in the entire draft wasn't there."

The Penguins, however, do not seem overly concerned with the cosmetic value of having Lemieux appear before the television cameras today wearing a black-and-gold uniform jersey. General manager Eddie Johnston is occupied with other matters.

The Penguins, who made trades that brought them the No. 9 and 16 selections in the first round of the draft — in addition to the No. 1 pick overall, which was already theirs — are one of several teams trying to lure the Los Angeles Kings into trading for the No. 3 choice. Johnston still feels the Kings will trade that choice and that the Penguins have the inside track if they do.

The reason for the increased interest in obtaining the No. 3 pick is the suspicion in the minds of some general managers and scouts that New Jersey is likely to squander the No. 2 choice. The Devils originally leaned toward taking Kirk Muller, a center from Guelph, Ontario, who played for Team Canada in the Winter Olympics. But the Devils now are believed to be tilting toward Ed Olczyk, a 6-1, 195-pound right wing from Chicago who played for Team USA.

The player the Penguins truly covet to complement Lemieux is Muller. But if they somehow succeed in obtaining him, they will increase the bargaining leverage of both Muller and Lemieux, because both are represented by the same agent, Gus Badali.

As of yesterday afternoon, Badali still was "advising the Penguins to leave (Lemieux) available for another NHL club because we're still so far apart in terms." And he warned that Muller's contract demands "will be very, very similar" to those of Lemieux.

But while Badali was doing his best to carve out the best deal for both players, Lemieux was telling reporters that he preferred to escape to the Penguins as opposed to the thought of being drafted by either the Montreal Canadiens or Quebec Nordiques, both of whom are anxious to obtain his services.

"There is too much pressure for a Quebec player to play here," Lemieux said. "That's why it's best I go to the United States."

Penguins GM Eddie Johnston and Lemieux after agreeing on contract terms in 1984.

In his Penguins' debut, Lemieux scores on his first shot

Pittsburgh	**2**	**1**	**0**	**—**	**3**
Boston	**0**	**2**	**2**	**—**	**4**

BY DAVE MOLINARI
The Pittsburgh Press

BOSTON — IT WAS, FOR THE better part of 29 minutes, sheer magic. But after 60 minutes, nothing remained except painful shreds of tattered illusion.

That there might be something special about this first game of the Penguins' 18th season was a thought worthy of consideration in the opening minutes of play, before many of the 14,451 denizens of Boston Garden had settled in their seats.

Just 1:18 after stepping onto the ice for the first time in his NHL career, Penguins center Mario Lemieux scored his first professional goal.

On his first shift. On his first shot. After relieving no less a figure than All-Star defenseman Ray Bourque of the puck. After faking Boston goalie Pete Peeters out of position with a move unencumbered by the limitations of most mortals.

But none of that really seemed to matter after the Bruins had rallied for a 4-3 victory in the season opener for both teams.

"All things considered, I'm happy," Lemieux said, his hushed tone and downcast expression betraying his words. "But it would have been better if we would have won."

That sentiment was echoed, if not amplified, by Penguins coach Bob Berry, who embraces a concept of a moral victory the way most people do an audit by the IRS.

"The score sounds good, 4-3, but I'm not satisfied with the effort," he said. "Not by a long stretch."

But if Lemieux and his teammates failed to earn a victory here for the seventh consecutive time, they did come away with a considerable amount of respect.

"I see these guys taking a run in the Patrick Division for that last — or maybe the third — playoff spot," Peeters said.

Should such a seemingly outlandish prediction be realized, he added, it would be largely because of Lemieux.

"He didn't do a lot tonight, but he still got a goal and I'm saying to myself, 'When this guy gets going, he'll be awesome.' He's going to flower after 30, 35 games, after he feels his way around the league."

Bourque, the victim of Lemieux's first professional grope, was understandably impressed after losing the puck and watching Lemieux skate 120 unimpeded feet before beating Peeters at 2:59 of the first period.

"I tried to pass the puck between his stick and his skate. It hit his skate and he was just gone. I think he's going to be a big help to that club."

That comment was illustrated by the Penguins' performance for the rest of the first period. They controlled much of the play and raised the lead to 2-0 at 13:53 when left wing Warren Young picked up a loose puck in the slot and rapped it behind Peeters.

The sellout crowd was dazed and

10.11.84

Boston's Pete Peeters is the first victim as Lemieux scores his very first NHL goal.

the Bruins were disorganized, but both conditions passed during the first intermission. The Bruins opened the second period with a swarming, relentless attack and the Penguins opted to try to protect their lead rather than expand it.

Goalie Denis Herron was able to hold off the Bruins until 8:13, when center Tom Fergus snapped a low wrist shot past him. The Penguins still had the lead, but had lost control of the game.

"We let the game go in the second period," Berry said. "We just started to back off and we played in our end almost the whole period."

Young managed to stun the Bruins — and delay the seemingly inevitable — 8 1/2 minutes later when he beat Peeters with a 45-foot wrist shot. The goal gave the Penguins a 3-1 lead and made this game as productive as Young's previous 20 in the NHL.

Still, Young entertains no thoughts of supplanting Quebec's Michel Goulet as the most prolific left wing in the game, although he might be the most candid.

"On the second goal I just had the puck and fired it on the net," he said. "I didn't know where it was going."

Thanks largely to Young's goal, it was difficult — at least briefly — to tell just where the game was going, but it was about to take a turn for the worse for the Penguins.

Ken Linseman's power-play goal at 18:56 put the Bruins back in striking distance and, just 38 seconds into the final period, they struck.

Dave Silk, operating in the left faceoff circle, threw a pass to defenseman Mike O'Connell, who was cutting down the slot. O'Connell knocked the puck behind Herron and it became apparent that nothing but the score was even.

Herron denied the Bruins with spectacular stops on Bourque, Silk and Nevin Markwart, among others, until 14:28, when Bourque cut across the top of the slot and beat Herron low on the glove side.

"I knew he was going to shoot it on the ice, because he shot high (on the previous shot)," said Herron, who finished with 32 saves and ugly welts on his collarbone and left hand. "At the same time he shot, someone fell on my leg. I was off-balance and by the time I challenged him, it was past me."

As was any chance the Penguins had of opening the season with anything but a loss. They managed a flurry of shots in the closing seconds and defenseman Moe Mantha was able to lift a shot over Peeters, but it came a full two seconds after time had expired.

10-10-85

“*He’s a young kid in a man’s world and sometimes ... things are difficult.*”

BOB PERNO

DEBUT NO. 2 FOR MARIO & PENGUINS

BY TOM MCMILLAN
Pittsburgh Post-Gazette

IT WAS ONE O’CLOCK IN THE AFTERNOON according to the clock in the grocery store down the street, and by this time a midsummer sun was broiling the concrete outside the Guy Gagnon Arena in Verdun, Quebec, Canada. Inside the arena, toes were freezing. ¶ Inside, where the thermostat had been dialed into the 30’s to keep the ice from turning to slush, the 10-year-olds of the Huron Hockey School were skating in circles the way pros do, learning stamina and patience, waiting for Mario Lemieux.

He is royalty in Verdun. He grew up a mile and a half away in a modest little duplex in Ville Emard, and he played at these very rinks as a boy, scoring a million goals if you count practice and warmups. The coaches had told the 10-year-olds that Lemieux, the National Hockey League’s rookie of the year in 1984-85, would stop by to shiver and shake hands and sign autographs. As they skated in their circles you could touch the excitement in the air.

“But you will not believe this,” Bob Perno said, climbing the steps of the bleachers at Guy Gagnon, frazzled. The big guy dumped on us!

“He is playing golf!”

Perno’s eyes narrowed. He and Gus Badali of Toronto have been Lemieux’s agents since Lemieux was 15 years old and the top midget draft pick in the province. In a sport that funnels its best players into the real world at 18, they have tried to teach him not to act his age.

“He knows better,” Perno said. “Do not say yes to someone unless you mean it. He would not do this kind of thing in Pittsburgh. Mario is really a very responsible guy, very dedicated. But up here, with family and friends

and everything, a lot of people want his time."

The next day, Lemieux is scheduled to drive to Ottawa to play in a golf tournament organized by teammate John Chabot. The next day, in the early morning hours, Perno is tapping at the front door of the Jean-Guy Lemieux residence in Ville Emard. "He is going to sign even if he is a day late," Perno says. "We are not going to let those little players down."

Lemieux dutifully rides in Perno's car to the arena, and he signs some autographs and makes the 10-year-olds' day.

"It has been a very busy summer, too busy," he says later. "But these are things you have to do. I must learn."

The education of a star resumes tonight at the Civic Arena, when the Penguins play the Montreal Canadiens in the first game of the second season of the Lemieux Era, something of a cut-rate Lemieux Debut.

They are going to pack the place to see him make the puck tap-dance. A year ago he became only the second player in hockey history to leap from Canadian junior leagues to the NHL and score 100 points, and he won the Calder Trophy as rookie of the year, and he was named the MVP of the All-Star Game. He has played 73 games as a Penguin and already ranks 35th in all-time scoring.

"And just wait," says Eddie Johnston, the Penguins' general manager.

"In the exhibition games I saw in Montreal, he was terrific — I mean, way better than last year. (Montreal general manager) Serge Savard said, 'Eddie, you always heard the guy was lazy, but he's not lazy anymore.' He's becoming a complete player. He's going to get a helluva lot of ice."

Lemieux was 2 years old when the NHL begat the Penguins in the fall of 1967; he turned 20 on Oct. 5, and already he is the most important player in the history of the franchise. When owner Eddie DeBartolo threatened to abandon town this summer, the Penguins dangled Lemieux's name in a series of radio commercials, teasing.

"Basically, we held him over people's heads," says Tim Rooney, the Civic Arena's vice president of advertising.

The marketing people sat down with Coach Bob Berry last month and plotted strategy for Lemieux's revised role in selling the team to the public; early last year, he spent less time on the ice than in the department stores, signing autographs, and Berry ranted.

"The kid is so willing to help us, and I think Bob understands our perspective now," Rooney said. "He came here from a place — Montreal — where marketing means going to the Giant Eagle. But we've never had an attraction here like Mario before, and we were like a ball and chain around Mario's leg. We'll 'fess up."

Lemieux signed a $600,000 contract after the Penguins drafted him No. 1 overall in 1984, a contract calling for two years plus an option, binding him to the team through 1987. Still, you look west into the Norris Division and see the Detroit Red Wings smashing the NHL salary structure to pieces, signing two unproven college free agents to $1 million contracts. You wonder what Lemieux and his people are thinking.

"Eddie Johnston has already come to us," Perno says. "We've got an offer on the table from the Penguins right now, which we are looking at."

Johnston, the general manager, and Paul Martha, the team's vice president, would like to make Lemieux a Penguin forever, and they would like to do it before the NHL Players Association gets the hang of free agency. Lemieux on the open market would be chaos. "Theirs is a good offer," Perno says, "but we've got to be careful about tying Mario up for a long time. We don't think any changes in the NHL's system of free agency will come about. But it's a possibility.

"On the other hand, I know Mario wants to stay in Pittsburgh."

Johnston added, "Mario is going to be here for a long time."

Lemieux went home to Ville Emard in the summer and played golf and sifted through endorsements and made a video — "Christmas for Kids" — with Paul Coffey of the Edmonton Oilers. He shopped for a condominium in Pittsburgh but decided to rent a house owned by Pierre Larouche, the former Penguin, who lives in Mt. Lebanon in the off-season. He rode a stationary bike and stayed away from sticks and pucks.

"The demands on him this summer were pretty heavy," Perno said. "I think he's looking forward to getting back to just playing hockey. He's a young kid in a man's world and sometimes all the outside things are very difficult. He's being asked to act like he's 28, or 30.

"But this is all a part of growing up."

Lemieux lived with the Mathews family — pictured are Nancy and son Michael — in suburban Mt. Lebanon during his first season in Pittsburgh.

Cooper

Happy holidays: four goals, two assists for Lemieux

Pittsburgh	3	1	4	— 8
St. Louis	1	0	3	— 4

By David Fink
Pittsburgh Post-Gazette

ST. LOUIS — BEFORE THE GAME, Mario Lemieux felt lousy. He was drowsy from the medication he had taken during a three-day battle with a cold and his legs were dead.

But when the firing subsided last night, it was the St. Louis Blues who felt sick after Lemieux shot their legs out from under them with a four-goal, two-assist explosion that sparked the Penguins to an 8-4 victory before a New Year's Eve gathering of 9,297.

It was the most goals and points in one game for Lemieux since he joined the Penguins last season. His performance overshadowed a three-goal, one assist outburst by fellow center Mike Bullard.

Mike Blaisdell scored the other goal for the Penguins, who are 5-3 in their past eight road games and 7-9-2 overall on the road. With the win, they tied their road victory output for the entire 1984-85 season. They also raised their record over Norris Division foes to an impressive 8-1-1.

Lemieux leads the team in goals (24), assists (42) and points (66). His six-point night pushed him past Montreal's Mats Naslund and back into second place behind Edmonton's Wayne Gretzky in the NHL scoring race.

Impressively, Lemieux scored on his only four shots.

Hampered by a cold, Lemieux nonetheless had a career night.

12.31.85

Afterward, Lemieux announced that he will sign a new contract sometime in the next week. Final terms of the deal, which is for one year plus an option, were worked out earlier yesterday in a meeting between Penguins general manager Eddie Johnston and Lemieux's agent, Gus Badali. So in a sense, this was Lemieux's way of saying thanks, not to mention Happy New Year.

"We're down to the last little details in the contract," he said. "I expect no further problems. I'm sure everything is all set."

The play began when rookie defenseman Craig Dahlquist, playing in his first NHL game, intercepted a clearing pass by St. Louis defenseman Ric Nattress. Dahlquist passed ahead to left wing Terry Ruskowski, who quickly dished to Lemieux.

The fun was about to start.

Lemieux, breaking down the left side of the slot, faked to his right, then moved to his left. Then, he faked to his right, slid the puck to his left, made a half-turn and slapped the puck past St. Louis goalie Rick Wamsley, who was helpless to stop it.

"That was the kind of goal," said St. Louis coach Jacques Demers, "that brings a standing ovation if you're playing at home.

"You can't compare Lemieux to Gretzky, they're too different in style, but what I saw out there tonight was Jean Beliveau (the former Montreal Canadien great). Beliveau could put you to sleep with the puck and then blast the goal past you. I know my game, and Lemieux's in Beliveau's league for sure."

Lemieux wasn't quite as impressed with his own performance.

"Hey, I wanted five goals after I got the first two to get me going," he said. "When things are going so good, why not go for it."

"It's nice when your big guns come through and get the big goals," Penguins coach Bob Berry said of Lemieux and Bullard. "They put on quite a show."

Quite a show, indeed, although they were almost upstaged by the Blues' third-period rally, which began when Penguins left winger Dave Hannan was given a five-minute penalty for high-sticking Bernie Federko.

FOLLOW-UP

Lemieux ended his second season with 141 points, second in the league. He led all Penguins players with 48 goals and 93 assists and received the Lester B. Pearson Award, given by the NHLPA to the league's best player.

Such a penalty, handed out only when the referee (in this case, Mike Noeth) believes there was intent to injure, does not end when a goal is scored. Trailing 5-1, the Blues struck quickly for two goals in a one-minute span.

First, former Penguin Ron Flockhart scored his second goal of the night and 12th of the season at 6:52, then Mark Hunter scored his 21st at 7:52. Bullard's second goal of the game and 20th this season interrupted the Blues' streak and restored the Penguins' lead to three goals at 6-3 at 9:03.

But Hunter scored again at 11:16 to make it 6-4.

Bullard completed his hat trick at 14:55 and Blaisdell added his 10th goal at 17:35 to wrap things up.

"A five-minute penalty like that can turn a game around so quick," said Berry.

Also overshadowed in the wake of Lemieux's performance was the brilliant goaltending of Roberto Romano, who faced a 21-shot onslaught in the third period, most of those shots coming with the Penguins shorthanded.

"Don't forget Romano," said Bullard. "He played a super game. They could've had a lot more goals during that five-minute power play."

The Blues had 15 shots in that five-minute span and finished the game with a lopsided 42-23 advantage.

"We cashed in almost every time we had a good scoring chance," said Bullard, who drove home three of his four shots. "That's what counts."

And that's why St. Louis was feeling, pardon the pun, so blue.

9.21.85

"And he's going to get stronger. I just think he'll get better and better."

EDDIE JOHNSTON

LEMIEUX: PITTSBURGH'S YOUNGEST STAR

BY DAVE MOLINARI
The Pittsburgh Press

LET IT NOT BE SAID MARIO LEMIEUX SLIPPED into town quietly, because his arrival two years ago spawned the sort of attention usually reserved for occurrences of much greater magnitude. ¶ A visit by the pope or the president, perhaps. Or something even larger, such as a quarterback controversy. ¶ He came with a modest command of the language, a thorough grasp of the monumental task before him and supreme confidence in his abilities. ¶ His attitude and aptitudewere routinely dissected, and there were those who projected him to be the final source of decay for a rotting franchise.

But, he has become, by almost universal proclamation, the world's second-most skilled practitioner of his craft, an athlete for whom the usual complement of adjectives is hopelessly inadequate.

And there is one other fragment of information necessary to put the Lemieux phenomenon into perspective: He will not reach the advanced age of 21 for two more weeks.

LEMIEUX'S ACCOMPLISHMENTS with the Penguins at this stage of his career dwarf those of even the most revered heroes in Pittsburgh sports. Consider that on their 21st birthdays:

◆ Roberto Clemente was in the midst of his first full season with the Pirates, during which he batted an undistinguished .255;

◆ Terry Bradshaw was about to enter his senior at Louisiana Tech, and was five years removed from National Football League stardom;

◆ Willie Stargell was preparing for his final season of minor-league baseball.

Of course, because of the junior-hockey development program, gifted hockey players traditionally turn professional at an earlier age than their counterparts in baseball, football and basketball.

As always, then, there is but one standard by which Lemieux's achievements can most accurately be measured: Wayne Gretzky.

Lemieux continues to pronounce Gretzky as the game's premier player — "He's the best ... he's still way up there" — but there is striking statistical similarity between their first two professional seasons.

Gretzky signed with the Indianapolis Racers of the World Hockey Association at age 17 and, after eight games, was sold to the Edmonton Oilers, who entered the National Hockey League the next season.

In those first two seasons — including one in the inferior WHA — Gretzky played in 159 games and had 246 points (96 goals and 150 assists).

Lemieux has played in 152 games in his first two NHL seasons and has 241 points (91 goals and 150 assists). Gretzky averaged 1.55 points per game his first two seasons, Lemieux 1.59.

Although Lemieux has a slight edge in that statistical comparison, Gret-

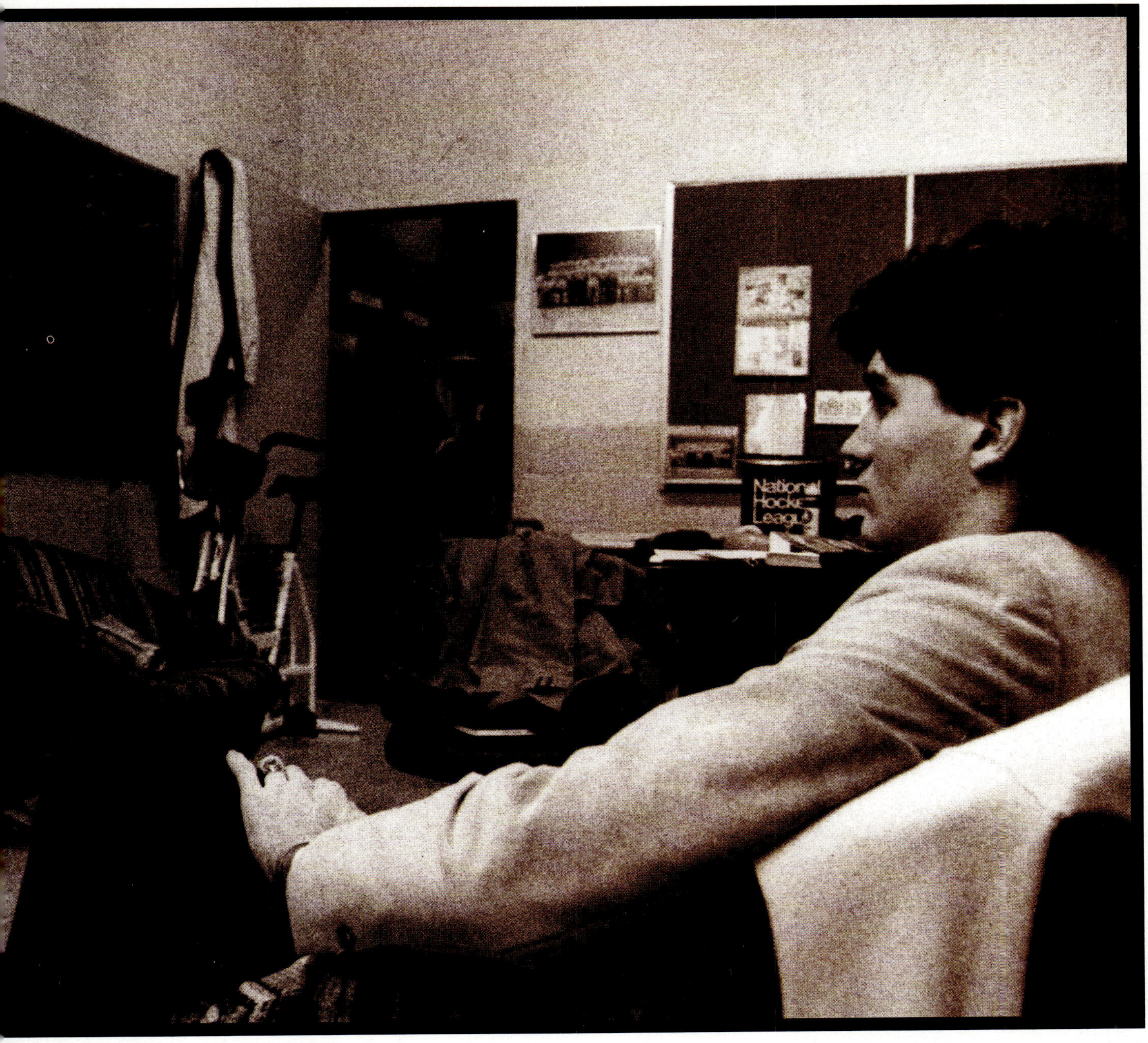

Lemieux studies game film at the Civic Arena in 1986.

zky possesses one critical attribute Lemieux lacks — the ability to approach every game, even every shift, as if it were the most meaningful of his career.

Lemieux, conversely, plays his best when his dominance is challenged, usually by an outstanding center such as Gretzky, Denis Savard or Dale Hawerchuk.

Put him on the same slab of ice as, say, the New Jersey Devils and only the sheer magnitude of his skills separates him from players of far less talent.

"It's just my concentration," Lemieux said. "Sometimes, it just lets me go. That's what I want to do — go out there and work hard every shift.

"I know that sometimes last year I didn't do it, because of many reasons. But if you want to be a great hockey player like Gretzky and Bobby Orr ... they went out and worked hard every

shift, and that's what I'm going to have to do to be as successful as those guys."

"I think that's something you develop," Penguins general manager Eddie Johnston said. "When Gretzky came into the league, he got better and better. Now, I think Mario will develop that."

There is one other significant difference between Gretzky and Lemieux. Gretzky carries 170 pounds on his 6-foot frame. Lemieux grew another three-quarters of an inch during the off-season, making him 6-5, and should play this season at 206 pounds.

Give Lemieux a decided advantage in wingspan and at least, theoretically, durability.

"And he's going to get stronger," Johnston said. "He's stronger this year. I just think he'll get better and better."

If so, Lemieux's popularity figures to increase accordingly, even though a newspaper poll last winter already showed him to be the city's most popular athlete.

Still, Ira Bass, the vice president and director of media for HBM/Creamer Inc. — while qualifying his observation as being strictly that of a fan — said Lemieux has not quite surpassed Steelers wide receiver Louis Lipps as the city's most recognizable athlete.

"That's because football is supreme here. Lipps is still No. 1 ... but Lemieux is close."

NO LONGER, HOWEVER, IS he merely the salvation of a franchise, but the prospective savior of a city's sporting pride. While the populace largely ignores the Pirates and mutters darkly about the Steelers, interest in — and enthusiasm for — the Penguins has reached an unprecedented level.

Season-ticket sales already have

generated about $3.2 million — some $1.2 million more than last year — and rampant talk of qualifying for the playoffs seems to be based more on reality than optimism.

Lemieux, more than any teammate, has experienced the trappings of success, both past and impending.

He has a contract worth more than $500,000 per year.

The North American media have chronicled his achievements in the most favorable manner possible, with only an occasional disparaging word.

Most of all, he has been exposed to the double-edged sword that is an integral part of celebrity.

Man about town: Lemieux serves a table of ladies during a dinner for charity in 1986 and jokes with the Pirates' Bobby Bonilla in 1988.

Lemieux's physical presence alone is enough to make him stand out in a crowd and his boyish handsome, chiseled Gallic features hold an obvious appeal.

He has, then, discovered that to venture into a public venue such as a restaurant or shopping mall is to solicit more relentless attention than he receives from any checking line.

"It's pretty tough because everybody knows the Steelers are not doing well and the Pirates are not doing well — and I think hockey's coming back real strong," Lemieux said.

WHILE LEMIEUX'S impeccable abilities have earned stifling attention from the media and public, he has been mainly ignored by companies seeking a high-profile spokesman for their products.

To date, Lemieux has received few endorsement offers. He promotes a car dealership here and hockey equipment in Canada, but his outside interests do not rival those of Gretzky.

"As his English becomes better and better, it's going to make him much more attractive to corporations," Bass said.

Gretzky has already achieved that level, at least in Canada. He has an agent, Michael Barnett, who handles nothing but endorsements, which include cameras, insurance, cereal and a Wayne Gretzky doll.

"If Mario played in Canada, his market value would rise immensely," said Bob Perno, an associate of Gus Badali, the primary agent for Gretzky and Lemieux.

"If Mario played in Montreal, it would be crazy. If he played in Toronto, where all the ad agencies are, it would be absolutely berserk," Perno added.

"Canadian agencies go after Wayne right away because he's the league's leading scorer, the MVP, and he's a Canadian boy playing for a Canadian team. Wayne has even had to cut back some because of overexposure."

In this country, however, Gretzky remains a decidedly minor figure, not to be confused with hustlers such as Pete Rose or Jim McMahon. That's because there are several overwhelming hurdles between even the most accomplished hockey player and nationwide recognition here.

The game is virtually ignored south of the Mason-Dixon line and the only nationwide coverage the NHL receives is on cable television.

"Attaining national recognition in the states is practically impossible because of the geographic considerations and contingent popularity," Toronto-based agent Billy Watters said.

"Mario is in trouble from that standpoint, that he'll never be a national hero. But since he plays in Pittsburgh, he has a much better chance than Gretzky playing in Edmonton."

"The time hasn't come yet, unfortunately, but there will be a time when hockey players are going to make it nationally," Ron Duguay, a former linemate of Lemieux's, explained. "I don't see how it can miss — it's such a great sport.

"It starts with little kids wanting to be hockey players. We will see it in time."

In the event that time rolls around in the next decade, Lemieux might well be the first hockey player to become a truly prominent national figure.

"Mario's a very bright person and, if put to the test, I think he would adjust," Duguay said.

"He can become someone like Larry Bird, who's very quiet but who's a real superstar and who does very well in front of the camera."

"What matters more than anything else is talent," Watters said. "And I don't think anyone doubts Mario has more than enough of that."

Lemieux has three goals, three assists in All-Star Game

Wales	1	3	1	1	— 6
Campbell	2	1	2	0	— 5

BY DAVE MOLINARI
The Pittsburgh Press

ST. LOUIS — NAMING THE PENguins' Mario Lemieux the Most Valuable Player in the NHL All-Star Game seemed an almost insufficient accolade.

So did the tribute from Edmonton Oilers coach Glen Sather, who coached the losing Campbell Conference team.

"I don't think we could have checked Mario with six guys tonight," Sather said after Lemieux led the Wales Conference to a 6-5 overtime victory at the St. Louis Arena. "He made it look so easy. We could have put a tent around him and we would have scored."

Lemieux was that spectacular.

He scored an All-Star record six points — three goals and three assists — with Lemieux's game-winning goal coming at 1:08 of overtime.

It was the first time anyone has scored more than four points in an All-Star Game.

"That was a scary performance," said Wales coach Mike Keenan.

It was a performance that left the standing-room crowd of 17,878 gasping at the ease with which he reduced the game's most prominent figures into bit players.

Lemieux said his play was less satisfying than his showing in the Canada Cup tournament. "Maybe in two weeks or 10 years this will mean more to me." But it left those who witnessed it groping for words to express their

Lemieux rides off with a new truck, awarded to the game's MVP.

2.9.88

admiration.

Consider his linemate, Montreal left wing Mats Naslund.

He set up Lemieux's three goals, but also picked up assists on two goals sculpted largely by Lemieux. Naslund finished with the second-highest point total in All-Star history.

"He's so good that I don't think it would embarrass any of my teammates to say he's the best player I ever played with," Naslund said. "It was nice to be involved with a record."

Said Lemieux: "I'd like to thank Mats Naslund for making great plays to give me a chance to score those goals."

The good times began when Keenan united Lemieux and Naslund at the Wales practice.

"That was a stroke of luck," Keenan said.

"That was a stroke of genius," Sather said.

Keenan said he played Lemieux with Naslund — first at right wing on a line with Quebec center Peter Stastny, then at center with Hartford right wing Kevin Dineen — because Naslund's speed and offensive instincts complement Lemieux's puckhandling skills.

Choosing Lemieux's most outstanding effort is difficult, but his first goal came closest to displaying the full range of his talents.

Lemieux lashed a shot at goalie Mike Vernon from the left faceoff dot, picked up the rebound, went around the far side of the net and tucked a shot inside the right post at 11:34 of the second period.

It was the type of goal he scores with seeming regularity for the Penguins, but a play few are capable of making.

"There probably isn't another man alive who could make that play," Sather said. "And he made it look so easy. Mario Lemieux was awesome. It's fun to watch him play."

Lemieux got his second goal when Naslund set him up at the left side of the Campbell net — "He's cool when he gets a scoring chance," Naslund said — and he merely waited for Vernon to make a move before snapping a shot over him at 8:07 of the third.

By then, Lemieux was receiving the sort of unrestricted ice time he has become accustomed to with the Penguins.

"When a player like that is hot, he doesn't feel any fatigue," Keenan said.

There certainly was no indication Lemieux was tired of scoring when Naslund slipped him the puck a little more than a minute into overtime.

Lemieux worked his way down the slot, moved the puck onto his backhand and stuffed a shot between Vernon's legs.

The goal culminated the second six-point game he has had at St. Louis Arena. The other came on Dec. 31, 1985. They are performances Lemieux already dreams of duplicating when the 1990 All-Star Game is at the Civic Arena.

"We have some of the best fans in the world. It would be nice to repeat this."

Who is going to say he cannot.

Lemieux nets franchise-record five goals

New Jersey	2	3	1	— 6
Pittsburgh	3	4	1	— 8

BY DAVE MOLINARI
The Pittsburgh Press

LOTS OF FOLKS ARE GIVEN TO excess on New Year's Eve. Most people get headaches for their trouble. Mario Lemieux got a piece of history for his.

Lemieux scored a franchise-record five goals and set up three others in the Penguins' 8-6 victory against New Jersey at the Civic Arena. His eight points tied the franchise record he set in a 9-2 victory against the St. Louis Blues on Oct. 15.

And although Lemieux's final point was of dubious pedigree — his shot appeared to enter the empty New Jersey net after time had expired in the third period — his performance was an authentic masterpiece.

"I think we all saw Mario's gift, a little late for Christmas, to me and the fans," Penguins coach Gene Ubriaco said. "I'm not going to say 'awesome.' I've said that too many times."

Which was fine with Rob Brown, Lemieux's right wing, who finished with a goal and three assists. "I think it was just another average night for him. He just decided this was going to be his game and nobody else's.

"Some of the things he did out there were amazing. They're going to have videotapes of tonight's game for kids to buy and watch, because it was just amazing.

"Even when he wasn't scoring goals, he was putting the puck through his legs, making twirls ... it

12.31.88

Lemieux tries to control an errant puck while holding back a defender.

was a classic example of the best hockey player in the world teaching us how to play."

The game did more than reaffirm Lemieux's status as the planet's premier player. It solidified the Penguins' grip on first place in the Patrick Division and kept them from going 0-for-1988 against New Jersey.

The victory was their first against the Devils in seven games (0-5-2) since Dec. 17, 1987. It also ended a five-game winless streak (0-4-1) against New Jersey at the Civic Arena.

But the two points the Penguins (23-12-3) earned were all but obscured by the eight Lemieux earned.

His assist on Brown's power-play goal 39 seconds into the second period was his 100th point in 36 games, the third-fewest a player has needed to pile up 100 points in NHL history.

Los Angeles center Wayne Gretzky, then of Edmonton, got 100 points in 34 games in 1983-84 and in 35 games in the next season. The Penguins have played 38 games, but Lemieux missed two in early November because of a wrist injury.

Lemieux scored three of his goals in the first period, the seventh time in Penguins history anyone scored a hat trick in one period. It was the fourth time Lemieux has done it.

He also tied the team record for most points in a period when he had a goal and three assists in the second. It was the fourth time a Penguins player has done that, but a career first for Lemieux.

Lemieux scored his goals in every conceivable manner. On a centering pass off defenseman Craig Wolanin's skate. On a slap shot from above the left faceoff dot. On a shot that dribbled between goalie Bob Sauve's legs. Into an empty net. And on a penalty shot against Chris Terreri, who replaced Sauve after the Penguins had scored on five of 10 shots.

Lemieux consulted Penguins goalie Tom Barrasso before the penalty shot, which referee Dan Marouelli called when Terreri threw his stick at the puck in the right faceoff circle.

"He (Barrasso) said he didn't know anything (about Terreri)," Lemieux said. "So I figured it out for myself."

That meant finding and exploiting an opening between Terreri's pads.

The Penguins' hold on first place would not have been jeopardized by a loss, but sustaining their first-place lead had to be comforting, especially considering a precedent set last season. The four teams — Detroit, Calgary, Montreal and the New York Islanders — leading their divisions on New Year's Day in 1988 went on to finish first.

But what must concern them is that, were it not for Lemieux's brilliant performance, this probably would have been just another depressing loss to the Devils. The Penguins were outshot, 35-19, and, for the most part, outplayed by the Devils.

"We didn't have a good game," Brown said. "Offensively, we played well but defensively we had our lapses."

"I feel bad for the players," New Jersey coach Jim Schoenfeld said. "They worked too hard, did too many things well, not to win. When you outshoot them almost 2-to-1 in their rink, the team that's in first place in our division ... "

His thought went unfinished, but the Penguins had no trouble tacking on an ending.

They recognized this was the latest in a series of victories that easily could have been defeats.

"Anytime you get 16 shots or whatever we had, you're not hitting on all cylinders," defenseman Paul Coffey said.

"We had a lot of people struggling right now," Ubriaco said. "Their spring has sprung for a little bit. They've overextended, and we've just got to get them back on their feet."

THE PENGUINS' PROBLEMS were particularly evident in their defensive zone, where New Jersey operated almost at will.

"They seemed to walk out of the corners against us, and I know we're stronger than them," Ubriaco said. "For some reason, we take guys at the wrong time ... we don't pin people. And it's not the biggest guys in the world who are coming out of the corners."

They came out of the corners and, more often than not, congregated in front of Barrasso, who made his 18th start in 20 games.

"We left Barrasso by himself a lot tonight," Brown said. "You can't do that, game in and game out."

Barrasso was beaten on five of 21 shots in the first two periods, but preserved the victory in the third with several superior saves.

"In the third period, Tom Barrasso just made up his mind they had enough goals on him, and he shut the door," Ubriaco said.

Only after Lemieux had opened another one wide enough for his team to slip through.

But although the Penguins realize they have been relying on individual bursts of brilliance, usually by Barrasso or Lemieux, to sustain them through this time of struggle, they offer no apologies for their good fortune.

"Hey, this organization has had so many bad times, I think it's kind of nice that we're having some good times," Ubriaco said. "And those who are looking to see us have bad times again, we're sorry. We still haven't had them."

FOLLOW-UP

Lemieux receives a special plaque as Dapper Dan Sportsman of the Year for 1988 at the Pittsburgh Hilton & Towers. It was his second Dapper Dan Award, having won the honor for 1986. He received a special Merci Mario award at the 1997 banquet, at which he officially announced his retirement and said that he would make his permanent home in Pittsburgh.

Peak playoff performance for Lemieux with five goals

Philadelphia	**1**	**2**	**4**	**—**	**7**
Pittsburgh	**6**	**3**	**1**	**—**	**10**

By Dave Molinari
The Pittsburgh Press

It was the kind of performance expected of Mario Lemieux. Predictable. Mechanical. Dry, bordering on dull.

Face it, the guy just can't talk a good game. Even after he has played one of the finest in NHL playoff history.

Lemieux tied an armful of league records with a five-goal, eight-point effort in the Penguins' 10-7 victory against the Philadelphia Flyers in Game 5 of their Patrick Division final at the Civic Arena. After a bit of prompting, Lemieux went so far as to say yeah, not only did he have a pretty good game, it might even rank among his best. Somewhere. Probably.

"It's tough to say. I've had a lot of great games, but under a lot of pressure like that — a key game for the team — I think that was one of the best."

Understand that eight-point games lost their novelty a while back; this was Lemieux's third since October. But it easily was the most productive game of Lemieux's brief playoff career — he had 10 points in the previous eight games — and came at a critical time.

The victory allowed the Penguins, staggered by a 4-1 loss in Philadelphia on Sunday, to regain control of the series. They lead, 3-2, and can clinch a berth opposite the Montreal Canadiens in the Wales Conference final with a victory in Game 6 at the Spectrum in Philadelphia.

But turning a team sport into a one-man tour de force is a notable achievement under any circumstance.

"He's elevated his game to the point where he just showed everybody else how much better than us he can be," Penguins goalie Tom Barrasso said.

"I've never seen a performance like Mario had tonight," Philadelphia coach Paul Holmgren said.

Few have, for Lemieux's accomplishments are almost without precedent in NHL playoff annals.

Until last night, New Jersey Devils center Patrik Sundstrom was the only player to get eight points in a playoff game.

Flyers right wing Tim Kerr was the only player to score four goals in one period and only eight had earned four points in a period.

Maurice Richard of the Canadiens, Darryl Sittler of the Toronto Maple Leafs and Reggie Leach of the Flyers were the only players to score five goals in a game.

Lemieux chiseled out a niche alongside all of them.

"It was just awesome," Penguins coach Gene Ubriaco said. "There's not much he can't do."

Not much he didn't do, either, from the time he beat goalie Ron Hextall on a breakaway at 2:15 of the first period until he pushed a Bob Errey pass into an empty net at 19:23 of the third period to close out the scoring.

It was the type of virtuoso performance expected of Lemieux since the playoffs began three weeks ago. Almost everyone figured it was coming, although no one knew when.

Lemieux freezes Philadelphia goalie Ron Hextall and scores easily during the first period. Left, he celebrates a third-period goal with Bob Errey.

"With a great player like Mario, it's only a matter of time," said Penguins defenseman Paul Coffey, who set a franchise playoff record with four assists.

Last night seemed an improbable situation because Lemieux was bothered by the effects of a neck injury he suffered in Game 4. On Monday, it was not certain he would be able to play. Twenty-four hours later, he played as few others have.

"Every time he gets banged or something, he seems to rise to the occasion," Errey said. "It sort of upsets him, gets him riled up a bit."

"The first shift, he had extra jump in him and you knew he was going to have a good game," said linemate Rob Brown, who scored two goals off Lemieux assists.

Hextall stopped Lemieux's first shot, but had no such luck on the next three as Lemieux recorded a natural hat trick in a span of 4:40, then set up Errey at 7:07 to make it 4-0.

"It takes Mario to lead the way, I guess," Ubriaco said. "And everybody

Coach Gene Ubriaco had many opportunities to congratulate Lemieux during this game. At right is Rob Brown.

just fell into place."

Everything appeared to collapse on the Flyers as Lemieux and Troy Loney added goals before the first period ended.

The Penguins never had scored more than six goals in a playoff game before. The outburst was the second-most productive period in playoff history. Montreal scored seven in the third period of an 11-0 victory against the Maple Leafs on March 30, 1944.

"We ran into a tremendous snowball with No. 66 on it," Holmgren said. "And when that gets rolling at you, it's tough to stop."

Being behind, 6-1, after the first period forced the Flyers to abandon the defensive style that is their forte.

"We can't run-and-gun with this team," Hextall said. Consider that a valid explanation for the Penguins' 9-3 lead after two periods.

The first two periods were the Penguins' best of the playoffs. They dictated the pace and consistently controlled the puck — on those infrequent occasions when it wasn't behind Hextall.

The final score suggests neither goalie was capable of stopping a medicine ball, but Barrasso absorbed a few comeback attempts with strong saves. He finished with 38 saves despite the swelling in his goals-against average.

"Hextall had his first bad game in two or three months," Coffey said. "And Tommy played great."

Philadelphia scored four of its goals in the third period, when the Flyers began opening arguments for Game 6, for they are a team whose heartbeat never flutters.

"They could have just packed it in and waited (for Game 6)," Brown said, "but they played good hockey."

One of the primary points made in that period is the Penguins' vulnerability when they stray from sound defense. But leading by nearly a touchdown could lull almost any team into defensive lapses.

"When you're young you see the finish line, like in a marathon," Ubriaco said. "You reach for the line instead of moving."

The Penguins nearly hit the wall before they reached the finish line. Philadelphia cut a six-goal lead to two with 2:37 remaining in the third period, injecting a significant measure of suspense into a game whose outcome appeared decided in the second period.

"Obviously, we didn't come out in the third and play like we did in the other two periods," Brown said. "It was poor on our part that we let them back in like we did because they still had a shot, but I think we controlled the game until the end."

The Penguins gained a tenuous grasp on this series, although it is premature to finalize travel plans to Montreal. The only thing the Flyers can be expected to concede is they are happy Game 5 is over.

LEMIEUX DRAWS OWN BOUNDARIES

BY BOB SMIZIK
The Pittsburgh Press

SEVERAL YEARS AGO HE CROSSED THE BOUNDary of the merely excellent and entered the realm of the truly great. And we thought we had him pegged, thought we comprehended the exact nature of his wondrous skills. He ceased to amaze us because we expected the incredible. And he produced it with regularity. ¶ He was the first- or the second-best player in the world. He was the first- or second-best player ever.

Pittsburgh never had seen the likes of him. The town never had an athlete dominate the sport the way he did. Not Clemente, not Stargell, not Bradshaw, not Greene.

But we knew that. And we thought we had seen it all.

We hadn't. The boundaries of Mario Lemieux's greatness were reshaped — again — at the Civic Arena against Philadelphia. From this experience, we must realize they will be reshaped again and again.

Sometimes we forget he is only 23, a young man who might be years away from his prime.

There was sincere doubt as to whether Lemieux would play against the Flyers in the Stanley Cup playoffs. Two nights earlier, in a collision with teammate Randy Cunneyworth, he injured his neck. His range of motion at practice the next day left doubt as to whether he could play, let alone play well.

Understandably, his teammates were concerned.

"I talked to Paul Coffey this morning," goalie Tom Barrasso said. "I said, 'Hey, it's going to be up to you and me and some other guys to take charge.' Fortunately, we didn't have to."

Didn't have to because Lemieux played like a man possessed, played like a man in the full bloom of perfect health, like a man who — incredibly — had something to prove, like a man who wants to be playing hockey well into May.

The Flyers blew seven goals past Barrasso, but the game never was in doubt. Never in doubt because Lemieux gave a performance that best would be labeled historic in this 10-7 victory that gave the Penguins a 3-2 lead in the best-of-seven series.

He scored five goals and had eight points. Four of his goals came in the first period, three came on successive shots within 4 minutes 40 seconds of each other.

The Penguins led, 5-1, at the end of the first period. Lemieux did that. He did it by beating Ron Hextall, one of the best goalies in hockey. He did it in the most crucial circumstances in which he has played — a playoff series deadlocked at two games. A loss would have put the Penguins on the brink of elimination with the next game on the road. Lemieux wouldn't let it happen.

"This was a big game. Mario would have had to be in a wheelchair not to play," said Bob Errey, Lemieux's left wing. "I don't know if I've seen him play any better. It's tough to play in the playoffs, obviously, and he really took it to them tonight.

"I knew he was ready to play. You could see it in his stride in the very first shift. He hadn't been getting behind a lot of defensemen in this playoff series. But you could see tonight he would. When his game is going and he's moving it doesn't matter if you put a checker on him. You can't stop him."

In eight previous playoff games Lemieux had scored 10 points. It would be an admirable pace for a normal player, but not for a man who has won two consecutive NHL scoring championships. There were 12 players ahead of him in scoring in the playoffs.

None of this was acceptable to Lemieux. More was expected of him. He knew it.

"Tonight there was something special about him," Dan Quinn said. "When he got out there in the first period he wanted the puck. And when he wants the puck it makes it tough for anyone to play against him."

He beat Hextall every which way. He did it on a breakaway, he did it standing beside the net on a perfect pass from Errey, he did it with his backhand, he did it with his forehand.

But best of all he did it by beating the bully goalie himself to the puck. Late in the first period Hextall exited the cage on his left side to go after a pass behind the net. Lemieux, coming from the other direction, used his long reach to beat Hextall to the puck. Once in possession he took the puck around the other side and poked it into the empty net.

It was history in the making. It was Lemieux at his finest, so superb a performance it seems unlikely to be duplicated. But we know better now. We won't be fooled again. You can't put limits on Mario Lemieux.

LEMIEUX
66
66
CCM

First-period hat trick gives Lemieux third All-Star MVP

Campbell	**2**	**2**	**3**	**—**	**7**
Wales	**7**	**2**	**3**	**—**	**12**

1.21.90

By Dave Molinari

The Pittsburgh Press

The game was less than 18 minutes old and already Mario Lemieux had one hand on the steering wheel and the hubcaps in his pocket.

Lemieux's first two goals had merely established him as the dominant player in the Wales Conference's 12-7 victory in the National Hockey League All-Star Game at the Civic Arena. The third of his four goals reaffirmed his place among the most spectacular performers in the sport's history.

In one blinding flash of skill, he seized possession of the Most Valuable Player's car (a Dodge Daytona) and captured the imagination of a continent.

You don't have to understand hockey to appreciate what he did. And no matter how well you know the game, there's no way to explain how he pulled it off.

Except to say he is Mario Lemieux, and that makes all things possible. Like being the first three-time MVP in history, despite playing in just five All-Star games. And completing the first-ever first-period hat trick in All-Star history with moves even the best players dare not dream of making.

Lemieux had carried the puck down the right side and was cutting toward the Campbell Conference net when defenseman Al Iafrate, all 6-3, 215 pounds of him, charged toward Lemieux. Lemieux dodged the check, pulled the puck around Iafrate and continued across the slot. He put the puck on his backhand, then flipped it past goalie Mike Vernon as defenseman Doug Wilson was knocking him to the ice.

The capacity crowd of 16,236 at the Civic Arena rejoiced. Lemieux smiled. And his peers, the finest players in the game, shook their heads. They couldn't believe what they had seen, but they couldn't doubt it, either. They've watched Lemieux for 5 1/2 seasons and realize that what is unthinkable for most is just an intriguing challenge to Lemieux.

"It was just phenomenal," Wales defenseman Raymond Bourque said. "The guys (on the bench) were looking at each other in awe. It was like, 'Wow.' "

"His third goal ... you've just got to laugh about it," Wales Conference defenseman Chris Chelios said, "because you only see a few guys in the league who can do that, and he can do it more often than most everybody."

When Lemieux scored at 1:07 of the third period, he joined Wayne Gretzky as the only players in All-Star history to score four goals in one game. Gretzky did it in one period in 1983.

Until the Wales squad scored 12, no All-Star team had reached double figures. For a time, it seemed Lemieux

Lemieux takes a breather during the Wales Conference's 12-7 victory in the 1990 All-Star Game in Pittsburgh.

While Lemieux provided the offensive fireworks for the Wales squad, Wayne Gretzky was ineffective for the Campbell Conference.

Lemieux, playing before a home crowd for the first time in his All-Star career, entered the game with a clear mandate: Make an indelible imprint on this game. Early. Often. The expectations were enormous. He exceeded them all, starting with the first shift.

"When I scored early, it took a lot of pressure away," he said. "Anytime you get a good start, you feel like getting a couple more."

Lemieux eventually got three more and might have tried for more if he realized Gretzky's goals record was so vulnerable. He passed up several scoring chances in the second period to set up linemates Propp and Cam Neely.

"When you get three in the first period, you think he's good for five or six," Neely said. "But he was a little concerned about trying to set up his linemates, and that shows a player who isn't selfish."

"A couple of times I should have shot," Lemieux said. "I made a couple of bad plays. I was little bit too generous in the second period. I could have had a couple more (goals), but sometimes that's the way it goes."

Yesterday, the game went whichever way Lemieux decided to take it. Pierre Turgeon and Kirk Muller scored two goals each for the Wales Conference and Luc Robitaille got two for the Campbell Conference, but no other player had nearly the impact of Lemieux.

Lemieux's skills were magnified by the lack of hitting in All-Star games. "I took advantage of that a little bit."

But that doesn't detract from his accomplishments. Not when his two consecutive NHL scoring championships prove it takes more than body contact to knock him off his game.

"I think he's proved that whether he gets hit or not, he can play in any type of situation," Chelios said.

"I don't think anybody let him do anything," Burns said. "He just went

might do that by himself.

He scored 21 seconds into the game, when he got the puck behind the net then swung around and threw a backhander inside the far post. At 13:00, he used Campbell defenseman Al MacInnis as a screen and beat Vernon with a slap shot from the top of the left faceoff circle.

Two shots, two goals and one amazing afternoon was taking shape. Lemieux figured as much when his second goal seemed to find the net purely by instinct.

"I never looked where I was shooting and it went in. So I knew then it could be a good day."

OK, so maybe the guy's a slow study. Just about everybody else needed far less time to know they were witnessing something extraordinary.

"Right from the first shift, he just took control," said Brian Propp, Lemieux's left winger.

"It took about as long to see that as it took him to score," Chelios said.

Lemieux's greatest moment of glory came at the expense of Gretzky, his archrival. Gretzky, the Campbell Conference's starting center, did not have a point and was on the ice for six Wales goals.

On a day when Lemieux was a supernova in a galaxy of stars, Gretzky's game receded into a black hole. But he still could marvel at Lemieux's brilliance.

"Even Wayne looked over and smiled one of the times he scored those goals," Wales coach Pat Burns said.

out there and took control."

Lemieux tortured Vernon, but there's nothing new about that.

He scored three goals against Vernon in the 1988 All-Star Game and routinely uses his long arms to stretch Vernon's 5-9 frame beyond its natural limits.

"He's a little small and I take advantage of that," Lemieux said.

"He's got the wingspan of a 737," Vernon said. "It's unbelievable. It's very effective and that's one of his biggest assets."

Vernon's greatest strength was his sense of humor and perspective. He knew the game didn't count in the standings, so he was just hoping his time in goal would disappear before the last trace of his pride did.

"I kept looking at the clock to see how much time was left. I said, 'Come on, keep it going.' "

By the time Vernon was replaced by Kirk McLean at 9:14 of the second period, he had given up eight goals on 21 shots. Lemieux was shooting 3 for 3 from the field and Vernon figured that entitled him to at least a fender of the car Lemieux won.

"That's twice now he's scored a hat trick against me and won the MVP. So you'd think he'd throw something my way, you know?"

Vernon and McLean probably wished they were in a different line of work yesterday. Something a little less hazardous, like being stuntman.

They had the misfortune of facing Lemieux when he wanted to make a point. When he was playing for his home crowd, the first network TV audience in the United States since 1980 and anyone who doubted the scope of his ability.

"You could sense that he wanted to perform really well," Neely said. "And naturally he certainly did."

"I got to show a lot of people that I was a good hockey player," Lemieux said. "That I could play with the best."

Or, more to the point, be it.

MARIO WOWS THE HOME CROWD

By Gene Collier
The Pittsburgh Press

Mario Lemieux, sensing the precise entertainment needs of a network television audience despite never having played to one, had his own agenda for the 41st National Hockey League All-Star Game.

There would be none. Instead, Lemieux planned an extension of Saturday's skills competition with his personal event.

Ladies and gentlemen, the slam-dunk contest. Funk on ice.

"I was surprised how big Mario is; he's like Michael Jordan in basketball," said Buffalo Bills quarterback Jim Kelly, who was among the 16,236 awestruck witnesses. "He's just one of a kind. It's guys like Gretzky, Jordan and Lemieux that makes sport what it is."

Perhaps, but this wasn't sport because it wasn't at all sporting to Mike Vernon, the poor man the fans voted to stand in the net for the Campbell Conference, the man who might next year campaign for someone else.

Cruising across home ice in the league's most opulent television spotlight in nearly 10 years. Lemieux was unchecked and unbelievable.

"He's got that big reach and he's just unreal," said Vernon, whom Lemieux tortures routinely, even under standard hockey rules, in which checking is not only allowed, but encouraged. "I thought I was in fairly decent position."

Lemieux had a record-tying four goals (a record fifth rang off the pipe), a record-setting three in the first period, one in the near-record-tying first 21 seconds. But the third was his signature goal, and the one that confirmed for everyone that this was his event and his alone.

He approached Vernon from the right faceoff circle, held off the Edmonton Oilers' Kevin Lowe with his left wing and swept the puck away from sprawling Toronto Maple Leafs defenseman Al Iafrate with his right, then tucked it in a microsecond past Vernon.

"I saw him (Iafrate) coming across," Lemieux said. "Everyone knows in All-Star games you're not going to get checked a lot. They're going to play the puck. I kind of took advantage."

Oh, yeah.

For this memorable afternoon, he was the antithesis rather than a peer of Gretzky, and because this was, technically, a competition, there had to be winners and losers.

Among the winners: Lemieux, forever most prominent, but include the city, the league for its ability to coordinate an entertaining weekend around a for-real network telecast, and Pierre Turgeon, the Buffalo center, who in his first All-Star Game displayed that he is an emerging monster among monster talents.

Among the losers, very few. Count NBC, which in all likelihood fought a losing battle in a nation that would sooner watch a college basketball game at 2 a.m. than a hockey game almost anytime. And count, unfortunately, Gretzky, who spent a long and dreary weekend doing a lot of curious stuff, including failing to show for Saturday's practice, disappointing a sell-out crowd, then getting despondent over the trade of good friend and teammate Bernie Nicholls.

> *I felt the pressure; I know people expected me to go out and win the MVP award.*
>
> MARIO LEMIEUX

Gretzky failed to score for the first time since he first appeared in an All-Star Game 10 years ago.

"Mario's at home, he scores on his first shift, that really gets him up," explained Lemieux linemate Brian Propp of the Philadelphia Flyers. But another factor, I thought, was that our line played Gretzky's line pretty well. We held them up. We played smart."

Wales Conference coach Pat Burns decided in the minutes before the game to match Lemieux's line against Gretzky's, and Lemieux seemed to delight in it.

"You're always surprised when Gretzky doesn't score," Lemieux said. "But anybody can have an off-night."

Sure, even in the day time, but The Great One?

Gretzky, a minus-6 for the afternoon, recoiled from every envy of Mario's big day.

"One of the biggest diseases we have in the world today is jealousy," Gretzky said. "If someone does well, you should be happy for them."

Pittsburgh is happy for Lemieux today, and he for it. His postgame remarks were peppered with appreciation for the city's support and gratitude for his ability to reward it.

"I felt the pressure; I know people expected me to go out and win the MVP award," Lemieux said. "The people of Pittsburgh deserve a lot. They've been supporting this team for a lot of years. I was just glad I was able to go out and give a little something back to them."

It is instructive that Lemieux is capable of such incredible doings in such highly scrutinized circumstances. He scored on his first shift in the NHL. He was the Most Valuable Player in his first All-Star Game. He won an All-Star Game with a goal in overtime. He won the Canada Cup in 1987 with two game-winning goals in the best-of-three series, one in overtime. He has done so many things that expand our expectations that even he has difficulty fulfilling them.

Great stages require great performers, and he is perhaps the greatest.

Severe back pains stop Lemieux's scoring streak at 46

Pittsburgh	**0**	**2**	**1**	**1**	**— 4**
NY Rangers	**0**	**2**	**1**	**0**	**— 3**

By Dave Molinari
The Pittsburgh Press

NEW YORK — OPPONENTS tried to stop Mario Lemieux for 46 consecutive games. Their methods varied, but the results didn't. They all failed.

But Lemieux's aching back betrayed him last night and did what no checking line or defensive shadow could: It prevented him from getting a point.

He took a regular shift in the first period of the Penguins' 4-3 overtime victory against the New York Rangers then worked only one shift and two power plays in the second.

And when the Penguins left their locker room for the start of the third period, Lemieux stayed behind. His run at Gretzky's record 51-game scoring streak was over.

He had been without a point in the first two periods eight other times in his streak, but managed to get at least one in the third period. Not even Lemieux can score from the trainer's room, however.

Lemieux, who has a herniated disc in his back, probably won't be scoring anytime soon, either. When his teammates flew to Winnipeg this morning, Lemieux headed back to Pittsburgh, where he was to be examined today.

Lemieux said he had "no idea" when he will play again; Penguins coach Craig Patrick said he hasn't "got a clue" when Lemieux will return, but said he expects him to miss at least the final two games of this road trip, in Winnipeg tomorrow and Chicago on Sunday.

Lemieux rests during the second period. He finished five games short of Gretzky's NHL record for scoring in consecutive games.

"He just really needs some rest," Patrick said.

The disk problem likely will require surgery, but Lemieux said he does not plan to have the operation now.

Lemieux clearly was disappointed his streak was over, mostly because the back condition denied him a rea-

2.14.90

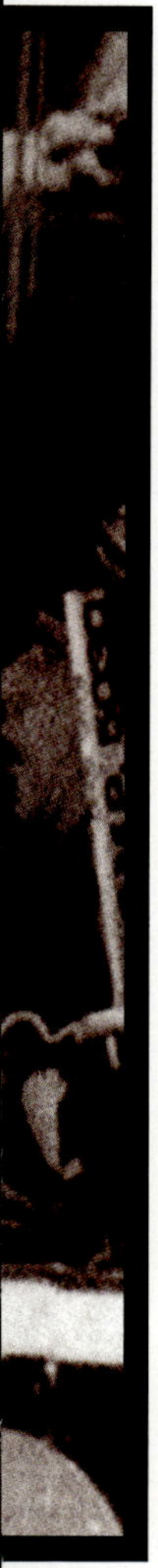

sonable opportunity to stretch it to 47 games.

"It's tough to not get a chance to get out there. It's tough to accept, but that's the way it goes."

"It just doesn't seem fair," said left winger Troy Loney, who scored the winner at 3:33 of overtime. "You hate to see it end because of an injury. That's what's sad. If the guy had been able to give his all tonight, he'd still have that streak going. We all know that."

Lemieux leads the NHL in scoring with 121 points on 44 goals and 77 assists. He had 39 goals and 64 assists during his streak, which began against the Los Angeles Kings on Oct. 31, 1989.

Lemieux came within inches of keeping the streak alive last night. The Penguins were on a power play midway through the second period when Lemieux passed to defenseman Paul Coffey, who moved it to center John Cullen. Cullen's shot caromed off the right goal post and Mark Recchi tucked the rebound into the net. Had Cullen's shot gone in, Lemieux would have received the second assist on the goal.

"We got the goal, and he's just as happy that we got the goal as (he would be) getting a point," Cullen said. "Mario said, 'Don't worry about me. We got the goal, and that's all that counts.' "

It was apparent long before that goal that Lemieux was struggling every time he stepped onto the ice.

"After the first period, he just said, 'I can't help the team,' " Patrick said.

"You could just tell on the bench he was really hurting," Recchi said. "He told me he couldn't even skate from blue line to blue line."

That's happened a lot in the past few weeks, when Lemieux's chronic back problems have flared up almost daily.

The pain almost prevented him from walking at times, but Lemieux refused to pull himself from the lineup.

"It's too bad it had to end this way, because he's really fought through this thing," Patrick said. "There have been a lot of games where he probably couldn't have played under normal circumstances."

"He's worked so hard and he's played through so much pain," Recchi said.

"He has done so much for us the past two months, played so well when there have been some mornings when he wasn't able to walk," Coffey said. "I know that in a lot of those games, he played because of the streak. But tonight, it just came to a head."

Lemieux allowed the streak to die only when he decided it would be counterproductive to the team's mission to try to extend it. He left the game after determining his presence would hinder more than help.

"He could have been selfish about the whole thing and tried to stay around for the third period to go out on the power play," Cullen said. "But he knew he wasn't helping the team. It got to a point where he just couldn't skate anymore."

"The streak doesn't matter at this point," Lemieux said. "I said I was going to play as long as I was able to help the team, and I wasn't able to do that."

So Lemieux has to settle for the second-longest streak in NHL history, but what he did remains a staggering achievement.

"That's something that players, except for Wayne Gretzky, can't even fathom," Cullen said.

But Lemieux does not operate within the game's conventional parameters. There is no guarantee he will duplicate this streak, but Coffey figures there's no reason to doubt he can.

"If he's healthy," Coffey said, "there's no reason he can't come out next year and do it again."

FOLLOW-UP

Back pain kept Lemieux off the ice for the next 21 games, costing him an 11-point lead in the NHL scoring standings. He returned to action for the Penguins' last game of the season, recording two points against the Buffalo Sabres.

Lemieux single-handedly dispatches Flyers

Pittsburgh	**2**	**1**	**0**	**— 3**
Philadelphia	**1**	**0**	**0**	**— 1**

BY DAVE MOLINARI
The Pittsburgh Press

PHILADELPHIA — THIS IS WHY the Penguins drafted Mario Lemieux first overall in 1984. Why they will pay him more than $2 million this season. Why they never will regret doing either.

In the Penguins' 3-1 triumph over the Philadelphia Flyers last night, Mario Lemieux didn't just make the win possible — he made it happen.

"Mario did everything you hear about him being able to do," Penguins center Bryan Trottier said.

Which is just about anything a hockey player can do. Lemieux scored all three Penguins goals — two on power plays, one short-handed — and turned in a performance so brilliant that goalie Tom Barrasso, who stopped 48 of 49 shots, was relegated to the No. 2 star.

So the Penguins (40-32-5) lead the second-place New York Rangers by two points in the Patrick Division and are one victory away from the championship that has eluded them since they entered the NHL in 1967.

Lemieux breaks in on Philadelphia goalie Pete Peeters and scores a shorthanded goal in the first period.

They secured home-ice advantage for the first round of the playoffs. They can clinch first place by beating the Detroit Red Wings tonight at Joe Louis Arena.

Lemieux is a quiet man whose visage rarely reflects his thoughts, but he virtually radiated intensity in the 36 or so hours before last night's game. His eyes were alive, his facial muscles taut.

"I've been thinking about these last four games."

He knew what he wanted and he knew how to get it. And there was almost nothing the Flyers could do to stop him.

Keith Acton's checking couldn't. The Flyers' taunts didn't work. Neither did the late hits and low blows that are staples of Philadelphia's strategy.

The Flyers were fighting to stay alive in the playoff race, but the odds on their survival plummeted when Lemieux took his first shift.

"Philadelphia has a lot of great role players," Penguins defenseman Gordie Roberts said, "but I know they wish they had a guy like Lemieux who can win games."

Lemieux gave the Penguins a 1-0 lead at 9:35 of the first period when he chased down a loose puck at center ice and beat goalie Pete Peeters on a breakaway. Craig Berube tied it for the Flyers 47 seconds later, but Philadelphia fell behind for good at 12:15.

3.26.91

Kevin Stevens helps Lemieux off the ice after Lemieux was hit in the face with a puck in the third period.

That's when Lemieux, killing an interference penalty against Kevin Stevens, stole the puck from defenseman Gord Murphy at center ice. He broke down the left side and backhanded a shot past Peeters for a shorthanded goal and a lead the Penguins never relinquished.

"We made two mistakes in the first period," Flyers coach Paul Holmgren said, "and a world-class player like that buries them."

Lemieux completed his hat trick at 10:30 of the second period when he collected a loose puck at the bottom of the left circle, spun and fired the puck behind Peeters to make it 3-1.

"With so much riding on it, for him to come up as big as he did was fantastic," Trottier said.

Lemieux left the game when he was hit above the left eye with a puck in the third period.

Lemieux at his best is like no one else in the game, which is why Barrasso's spectacular performance was largely overlooked. Philadelphia got the game's first eight shots and outshot the Penguins, 49-21, but picked up its only goal when Berube knocked in a loose puck after a four-on-two break.

"You can't ask much more from Tom Barrasso," Penguins coach Bob Johnson said. "That's the way we want him to play. That's the way he's got to play."

GAMES WE WON'T FORGET

Lemieux's goal outshines the Stars

Minnesota	0	1	0	— 1
Pittsburgh	2	2	0	— 4

After slipping past two defensemen, Lemieux falls to the ice and scores the game-tying goal against Jon Casey. "You could just see the determination when he picked up the puck," Penguins left winger Bob Errey said.

BY DAVE MOLINARI
The Pittsburgh Press

AT SOME POINT IN THE distant future, Mario Lemieux might try to tell his grandchildren about this goal. He won't do it justice.

No words can capture how he made the near-impossible look so easy, so natural. The play could not be defended, let alone described. It should just be savored for the way it demonstrated Lemieux's gift for this game.

And for how it might have preserved the Penguins' chances of winning the Stanley Cup.

The goal Lemieux scored at 15:04 of the second period during the Penguins' 4-1 victory against the Minnesota North Stars in Game 2 of the Cup finals at the Civic Arena last night was the type of play on which a series can turn.

At the very least, it has enabled the Penguins to go to the Met Center for Game 3 tomorrow with the series tied, 1-1.

Had the North Stars won Game 2 — a very real threat before Lemieux scored — Minnesota would have had a chance to close out the series before it could return to the Civic Arena for Game 5.

"Obviously, this was a game we had to win," Penguins coach Bob Johnson said.

Just as obvious: the 2-1 lead the Penguins had late in the second period was tenuous, at best. The North Stars were slowly building momentum and seemed poise to take control of the game.

"It was anybody's game at that point," Penguins forward Randy Gilhen said.

But it became Lemieux's when he got the puck at the top of the circle in the Penguins' zone, carried the puck down the middle of the ice, slipped

5.17.91

between defensemen Neil Wilkinson and Shawn Chambers, and flipped a backhander past North Stars goalie Jon Casey while falling to the ice.

"You could just see the determination when he picked up the puck," Penguins left winger Bob Errey said.

"A great play by a great player," Johnson said.

And a deflating one for the North Stars, who gave up another goal to Kevin Stevens 1:28 later. They had seen 35 minutes of fairly solid hockey negated by Lemieux's burst of brilliance.

"When he does something like that, it just lifts our whole team," Gilhen said. "That goal kind of broke things open for us."

"He's got to come up with those big plays," left winger Phil Bourque said. "And he picked the right time to do it, because we needed a lift. They were coming at us."

This was the type of goal then-General Manager Eddie Johnston envisioned Lemieux scoring when he drafted him in 1984, the kind the Penguins have come to expect from perhaps the most menacing offensive player in the history of the game.

"That's why they pay me a lot," Lemieux said.

They couldn't pay him enough for what he did in Game 2, but Lemieux was not the only one who turned in an honest evening's labor for his paycheck last night.

There was goalie Tom Barrasso, who stopped 39 of 40 shots; Stevens, who ended a two-game scoreless streak with two goals; the penalty-killers, who shut down Minnesota's power play eight of nine times; and defenseman Paul Coffey, who gave the Penguins an emotional jumpstart by

In the locker room, Lemieux hoists the Penguins' first Stanley Cup in team history.

playing for the first time since April 20, when his jaw was broken.

The North Stars outshot the Penguins 40-31, but got their only goal when Mike Modano swatted in his own rebound during a power play 55 seconds into the second period. Minnesota put a few shots of dubious pedigree behind Barrasso in Game 1, but his performance last night was virtually flawless. This was the first time Minnesota has been limited to one goal during this year's playoffs.

"He got a lot of work, and he responded very well," Johnson said. "He gave us a great game. When you get to this point, you need great goaltending."

The Penguins have gotten that from Barrasso throughout the playoffs, even though he tried to deflect much of the praise he received last night.

"Our defense is a team defense, and I've got my role to fill. When we play like we did tonight, we're getting performances from everyone, not just individuals."

The Penguins played with an urgency missing in Game 1. They finished checks, pursued every loose puck and acted like a team that recognized the gravity of its predicament.

"They were a little more desperate tonight," North Stars forward Stewart Gavin said.

And a lot more emotional. The Penguins play better when they dislike their opponent, and they seem to have cultivated a healthy distaste for the North Stars.

Lemieux stole whatever jump the North Stars had when he scored his spectacular goal. The one that kept Penguins in this series. The one that might have made a Stanley Cup possible.

"It's great to see him get the goals when the team needs them," Stevens said. "He's a big-time player."

5.28.91

Mario Lemieux holds the Stanley Cup aloft before 80,000 fans at Point State Park in Pittsburgh.

RGH PENGUINS

GAMES WE WON'T FORGET

Lemieux rides to the rescue in brilliant fashion

Washington	2	0	2	— 4
Pittsburgh	1	4	1	— 6

BY DAVE MOLINARI
The Pittsburgh Press

THE PENGUINS COULD HAVE been in a more precarious position heading into Game 3 of their Patrick Division first-round playoff series against the Washington Capitals.

It's just hard to imagine how.

They had a 2-0 deficit against one of the finest teams in hockey and their first-line right winger, Rick Tocchet, was out with a bum shoulder. Being beaten and beaten up is not a pleasant combination.

But just when it looked up as if the Penguins needed a minor miracle, they got something even better: a major Mario. Which turned out to be more than enough, thank you.

Mario Lemieux set up the Penguins' first three goals and scored the final three in their 6-4 victory against the Capitals at the Civic Arena, slicing Washington's lead in this best-of-seven series to 2-1. And reminding everyone of how Lemieux is a threat to redefine his own brilliance every time he goes over the boards.

"It's ridiculous, some of the things he can do," Penguins left winger Kevin Stevens said.

Which is to say, just about anything at almost any time.

"He did pretty much what he wanted to do out there tonight," Washington coach Terry Murray said.

Consequently, Lemieux is pretty much the reason the Penguins can go

4.23.92

into Game 4 tomorrow intent on tying this series instead of just delaying their departure from it.

"I wouldn't have been too optimistic if we'd lost tonight," defenseman Larry Murphy said.

That's understandable, considering only two teams in National Hockey League history have rallied from 3-0 deficits to win a series. And that nobody has pulled it off against a team as accomplished as the Capitals.

Even now, the Penguins hardly are an odds-on choice to reach the second round: Only 20 teams have overcome 2-0 deficits to win a series since the NHL adopted a best-of-seven format in 1939.

"I don't think that in a seven-game series, you can ever get carried away with one game," right winger Joe Mullen said. "We've got to win three more, and we know it's a tough haul."

But it has to be reassuring to know how Lemieux is around to carry so much of the load. The Penguins have gotten eight goals in the past two games; Lemieux made the passes that led to five of them and the shots that accounted for the other three.

Last night, Lemieux downplayed personal achievements and talked about the importance of having 20 players work toward a common objective. There's nothing wrong with that, so long as one of them is a lanky guy who wears No. 66 and plays the game at a level most players cannot comprehend.

Statistically, this does not qualify as the best playoff game of Lemieux's career. He had five goals and three assists in a second-round game against the Philadelphia Flyers on April 25, 1989.

Lemieux usually thrives under the pressure of critical games — a cursory check of his resume from Canada Cup and playoff games prove that — but there were some early doubts about whether his teammates would do the same last night.

COACH SCOTTY BOWMAN SAID the Penguins were primed and "ready to chew nails," but those in the capacity crowd of 16,164 likely were gnawing on their fingernails in the opening minutes of the game. The Penguins were sluggish and tentative at the start.

"In the first few minutes of the game, they were kind of sitting back, waiting for something to happen," Murray said.

They didn't have to wait long. The first period was one minute, 33 seconds old when Washington defenseman Kevin Hatcher scored a shorthanded goal on a two-on-one break with Mike Ridley.

"We got off to kind of a shaky start with the short-handed goal," Bowman said. Had it been any shakier, seismologists might have flocked to the Civic Arena.

But the Penguins righted themselves when Lemieux set up Phil Bourque at the front edge of the crease at 6:27 and retained their composure even after Dimitri Khristich gave Washington a 2-1 lead at 17:47.

"I'm not as much concerned about how you start as how you finish," Penguins goalie Tom Barrasso said. "And the finish looked pretty good to me."

This one had a happy ending for the Penguins because Lemieux set up goals by Mullen and Jaromir Jagr in the first half of the second period, then scored two before the intermission.

The shot he tapped past Capitals goalie Don Beaupre during a five-on-three power play at 19:07 proved to be the game-winner, but only because the Capitals surged in the waning minutes of the third period. Al Iafrate and Hatcher got Washington to within a goal, 5-4, after much of the crowd had headed for the parking lot.

"We fell asleep," Lemieux said. "The last five minutes of the game, we stopped skating and putting the pressure on their 'D.' And with the personnel they have back there, you can't do that."

It fell to Lemieux to abort Washington's comeback. At 19:09, he stretched to swat down a Hatcher clearing pass in the Capitals' zone, then pushed the puck into an empty net to make the outcome official.

It was a fitting end to a game that had Lemieux's signature scrawled all over it. The empty-netter was his easiest point of the night, but there aren't many freebies against Washington. The Capitals can play defense with a passion, and containing Lemieux is always a priority.

"The last half of the year, we've used two lines and we've used four different lineman against him," Murray said. "And still, sometimes that's not good enough."

GAMES WE WON'T FORGET

Lemieux's late goal gives Penguins second Cup

Chicago	**3**	**1**	**0**	**— 4**
Pittsburgh	**1**	**2**	**2**	**— 5**

BY TOM MCMILLAN
Pittsburgh Post-Gazette

CHICAGO — IT WAS THE classic matchup — or so the NHL thought.

The grit and defensive tenacity of the Chicago Blackhawks against the speed and finesse of the Penguins in a best-of-seven series for the Stanley Cup. "Could be one of the great finals ever," said TV analyst John Davidson, voicing the prevailing opinion.

But the favored Penguins would turn it into a rout, annexing their second straight Cup in four straight games, including the last two at that creaky, intimidating barn, Chicago Stadium.

Last night, in the series clincher, Mario Lemieux scored on a power play with 12.6 seconds left in the game to give the Penguins a 5-4 victory.

The Penguins won different games in this series with different styles — a blur of up-tempo offense, a clinic of tight-checking defense. When the Hawks hit, the Penguins hit back. Harder. When the Hawks skated, the Penguins skated with them. Faster.

"It wasn't as lopsided as it seemed," Chicago coach Mike Keenan tried to protest later, arguing that three of the games had been decided by one goal.

But the Penguins seized control of the series from the time they erased a three-goal deficit in the second period of Game 1, and the only question after that was whether it would be the first sweep of a series since 1988.

"Give them credit," Penguins winger Rick Tocchet said with proper respect after the Hawks had been vanquished. "They kept coming at us."

It was a confident Chicago team that rumbled into Pittsburgh for Game 1, riding a playoff-record 11-game winning streak. The Blackhawks had swept Detroit in the Norris Division finals, then blown out Edmonton in four games in the Campbell Conference finals, and there was bold talk of Chicago's first Cup since 1961.

The confidence was understandable when they exploded for a 3-0 lead in the first 13 minutes of the opener, and kept battling fiercely to make it 4-1 in the second period. But the Penguins — showing the resilience that has been their trademark — roared back.

Jaromir Jagr tied it on a breathtaking move off the left-wing boards in the third period before Lemieux's game-winner on the power play. The Penguins merely winked about the good fortune of their 5-4 victory. The Hawks — derailed — were stunned.

"It's inexcusable to give up a three-goal lead," Keenan seethed.

Playoff MVP Lemieux has the look of a champion upon meeting the press with the Conn Smythe Trophy at his side.

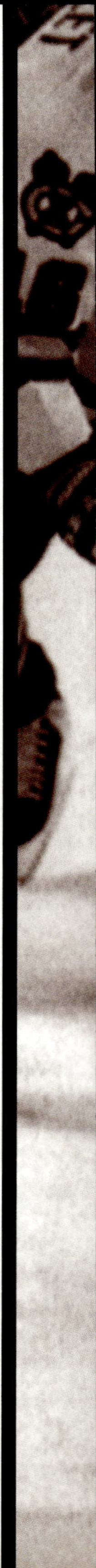

5.26.92

CALL YOUR
CABLE COMPANY

Right now, we're living in Mario's world.

BRYAN TROTTIER

THE MAN OF THE MOMENT IS MARIO

By Tom McMillan
Pittsburgh Post-Gazette

THE SCENE WAS THE WALES CONFERENCE finals of this year's NHL playoffs. One of the best defensive players in league history had just faced one of the best offensive players. ¶ "He's the best player in the league, if not the best ever to play the game," Ray Bourque said of Mario Lemieux. ¶ High praise, indeed, from Boston's All-Star defenseman, but not gushingly inaccurate words from a vanquished foe. ¶ *Le Magnifique* began this latest bid for immortality by almost-single-handedly dragging the Penguins to victory in their first-round series against Washington, scoring an outrageous 17 points in six games. The defending NHL champs rallied from a 3-1 deficit to eclipse the Caps with three straight wins, two of them in Landover, Md. Washington coach Terry Murray — and his players — stood in utter amazement.

"We were beaten by one man," Murray said. "No. 66. Lemieux. Right now, he's the best there is ... by far the the best player in the NHL. And he's on top of his game. He's a guy the puck just follows around the ice."

Al Iafrate, who spent much of the series hounding Lemieux, put it this way: "He's gifted. He's big. He's tough. He's the man."

Lemieux was on pace to shatter Wayne Gretzky's single-season playoff scoring record until Adam Graves sent him crumbling to the ice with a vicious slash in Game 2 of the Patrick Division finals against the New York Rangers. But the Penguins persevered, roaring through adversity to oust the Rangers in six games, and then taking a 1-0 lead over Boston ... and then Lemieux returned.

It was magic.

"Right there the series changed," Boston coach Rick Bowness said. "All of a sudden, we were in awe."

In Game 4, on what was probably Lemieux's most spectacular goal of the playoffs, he broke out shorthanded, virtually skated up Bourque's back, slipped the puck between Bourque's legs, and snapped a shot over flailing goalie Andy Moog.

"So big, so strong," Bourque

Lemieux is the center of attention as he talks with reporters in the locker room following the Penguins' four-game sweep of Chicago in the 1992 Stanley Cup finals.

marveled. "Right now, he can do whatever he wants."

Having swept the Bruins, Lemieux and the Penguins faced the challenge of the Chicago Blackhawks, arguably the best defensive team in hockey.

No problem.

Lemieux snapped in two goals in each of the first two games at the Civic Arena as the Penguins grabbed a 2-0 series lead.

He scored the dramatic winner in Game 1 on a power play with 12.6 seconds to play. The great ones find a way.

"And now we've got to find a way to deal with him," Chicago coach Mike Keenan said. "We've got to come up with a better plan."

They didn't. Lemieux and the Penguins played astonishing defense to gut out a 1-0 victory in Game 3 at Chicago Stadium. In Game 4, Lemieux had a goal and two assists to lead the Cup-clinching, 6-5 win. The big man was everywhere, deking defensemen, terrorizing goalies. Even after goaltender Dominik Hasek stopped him on several breakaways in the final game, Lemieux smiled and said, "Don't worry, I'll get him next year."

All that was left for the league to award the Conn Smythe Trophy, and there was no suspense — except in Lemieux's mind. He thought the honor should have gone to goaltender Tom Barrasso.

"I thought it was Tommy all the way," Lemieux said. "I missed six games, remember? And Tommy was superb all the way."

The Smythe voters disagreed. Despite Lemieux's injuries, he led the NHL in playoff scoring with 16 goals and 34 points in 15 games. And he tied a league record with five game-winning goals.

That second Smythe will look sparkling next to the second Cup.

"We salute them," Keenan said. "They've got a great team, great talent, great coaching. A good mix of youth and experience. And the best player in the game."

The Penguins could not have done any of this without their role players, their muckers, their grunts. Jock Callander came up from Muskegon to score a key goal in the Boston series. Dave Michayluk played his first NHL game since 1983. Gordie Roberts offered steady, reliable defense. Bob Errey banged around with a separated shoulder.

But this team will be remembered for its star quality, its elegance, its greatness — and, ultimately, for Lemieux.

"If I had to describe him in two words, they would be these: only perfect," teammate Bryan Trottier said. "Right now, we're living in Mario's world."

1.13.93

LEMIEUX TO MISS 4-6 WEEKS WITH HODGKIN'S DISEASE

DISCOVERED EARLY

RADIATION TO BEGIN

PROGNOSIS IS GOOD

'NO THREAT TO LIFE'

"*Any time you're talking about cancer, you're worried.*"

BOB ERREY

BY DAVE MOLINARI
Pittsburgh Post-Gazette

MARIO LEMIEUX IS EXPECTED TO BE out of the Penguins' lineup for four to six weeks while undergoing radiation treatment for Hodgkin's disease, a form of cancer described as "no threat to life, no threat to his career." ¶ Penguins owner Howard Baldwin said the optimistic prognosis is the byproduct of discussions with "every doctor we've spoken to." ¶ The Penguins announced last night that Lemieux, 27, was diagnosed with Hodgkin's disease after doctors removed an enlarged lymph node from his neck. ¶ Tests showed the disease, which usually affects people between the ages of 15 and 35, was caught in an early stage. When detected early and treated with radiation therapy, 90 to 95 percent of the cases can be cured. ¶ "It was caught so incredibly early," Baldwin said. "If you catch it early, it's so non-threatening they don't even keep statistics on it."

Lemieux, who leads the NHL in scoring with 104 points, was sidelined by back pain last week. But Baldwin said the Hodgkin's disease only was diagnosed "within the past 72 hours."

The cause of the disease is not known.

Baldwin, Lemieux and Penguins general manager Craig Patrick are scheduled to brief reporters on Lemieux's condition Friday at the Civic Arena.

"His attitude is incredible," Baldwin said. "He's ready to go. He's in great form."

Earlier yesterday, Lemieux's teammates made their annual visit to Children's Hospital, but Lemieux was not present.

"Any time you're talking about cancer, you're worried," winger Bob Errey said. "You have to trust what the doctors are saying and be positive."

Lemieux's agent, Tom Reich, issued a statement from his California office saying, "He has a condition ... that is in a mild stage. The prognosis is extremely good."

For the past five years, Lemieux has been the honorary chairman of the Pittsburgh Cancer Institute.

A young fan adds his get-well wishes to his hero, Mario Lemieux, to a giant card filled with signatures.

We Love You, Mario - Get Well

PLAYERS STUNNED, HOPEFUL

MARIO VISITS TEAM

BY DAVE MOLINARI
Pittsburgh Post-Gazette

PENGUINS GOALIE TOM BARRASSO KNOWS all about cancer. He watched his daughter, Ashley, beat some staggering odds to survive a bout with it less than three years ago. ¶ So yes, Barrasso was stunned when he heard teammate Mario Lemieux had been diagnosed with Hodgkin's disease. But he quickly established Lemieux as a prohibitive favorite to win this battle with the disease. ¶ "I think that while the initial shock (of a cancer diagnosis) is always a great one, as time goes by this will be more of an annoyance to him than any grave danger to his health," Barrasso said. ¶ That might be overstating it a bit, but doctors believe Lemieux's cancer was detected early and confined to an enlarged lymph node that was removed from his neck. ¶ Lemieux visited with his teammates briefly at the Civic Arena yesterday, and told reporters he is optimistic about his chances of recovery. "I'll be fine," he said. "No problem."

Dr. Charles Burke, the Penguins' team doctor, briefed the players on Lemieux's condition and prognosis after practice yesterday. He emphasized the cure rate of more than 90 percent and the importance of diagnosing Lemieux's condition when it was in an early stage.

"The particular disorder he's been found to have has a tremendously high rate of success in being cured, and he's got to feel good about that," Barrasso said.

Cancer is the latest entry on a long list of medical problems that have imperiled Lemieux's career since he entered the NHL in 1984. His chronic back troubles have gotten most of the publicity, but Lemieux has endured numerous other maladies.

"It just seems that everything keeps coming down on him," left winger Kevin Stevens said.

The Penguins believe that all the adversity Lemieux has overcome en route to becoming hockey's most dominant player has prepared him to cope with the greatest challenge of his career. And his life.

"It throws you a little bit when you see something like this happen to him, but knowing the kind of person he is and everything else, you feel he's going to come through it all right," center Ron Francis said.

Lemieux told the Penguins that's precisely the approach he's taking.

"He's upbeat about it," Stevens said. "He's positive everything's going to be fine. The doctors say it's almost 100 percent that everything's going to be fine."

SUCCESS TOO GOOD TO LAST

PENS CURSED AGAIN

By Bob Smizik
Pittsburgh Post-Gazette

We should have expected this, should have known everything had been going too good for too long. ¶ We should have realized these were the Penguins and misfortune is always lurking, always ready to pounce. This is a team that for the greater part of 26 years has been too familiar with staggering injuries, monumental incompetence, incredible bad luck and yes, even death. ¶ Whenever things started to go bad, too quickly they went bad. ¶ Sure, there have been two consecutive Stanley Cup championships. But they were wrapped around the slow death of the beloved Bob Johnson. ¶ And now this. In the midst of what loomed as their greatest season — when this assortment of wondrous talent came together not merely as a team to be reckoned with in the postseason but one capable of dominating the league — their greatest player has been struck down. Again.

Mario Lemieux is suffering from Hodgkin's disease. It is cancer at its most treatable, at its least lethal.

But it is cancer.

The odds, the doctors tell us, are greatly in Mario's favor. Recovery is said to be more than 90 percent. The best prognosis is Lemieux will miss about six weeks while undergoing radiation therapy.

Lemieux's assault of Wayne Gretzky's scoring record, as recently as two weeks ago seemingly achievable, is no longer of importance. Neither is the team's quest for a third Stanley Cup.

The man who is, arguably, the greatest athlete in Pittsburgh sports history, finds his career in jeopardy for the second time in less than three years.

It was less than 35 months ago that back surgery on Lemieux was considered "career-threatening."

He came back from that to achieve what most had considered impossible. He played with even more skill than he had prior to the surgery.

The body of medical opinion is comforting in Lemieux's latest medical crisis. Not only is Hodgkin's eminently beatable, but Lemieux's youth and vigor make him even a better candidate to return to the ice by the end of next month and lead the charge to another championship.

Should that happen, should even another championship be won, expect no one to suggest this will be a team that will live happily after.

GAMES WE WON'T FORGET

Lemieux returns from cancer — and scores

Pittsburgh	**1**	**3**	**0**	**— 4**
Philadelphia	**3**	**1**	**1**	**— 5**

BY DAVE MOLINARI
Pittsburgh Post-Gazette

PHILADELPHIA — IF YOU APPLY Mario Lemieux's normal standards to this game, it might look as though he had a pretty lousy evening.

Two points? Against a last-place team? In a loss?

But this was not just any other game. There were some circumstances that merit consideration when analyzing Lemieux's performance during the Penguins' 5-4 loss to the Philadelphia Flyers last night.

Less than 12 hours before game time, Lemieux was being subjected to blasts of radiation designed to knock any lingering traces of Hodgkin's disease out of his body.

So considering Lemieux began the day as a cancer patient, maybe getting a goal, an assist and playing about 21 minutes wasn't such a bad night's work, after all.

"It's unbelievable," Penguins left winger Kevin Stevens said. "It's crazy. How can you even imagine what he did tonight? There's only one person in the world who could do it, and it's him."

"He's an amazing athlete," Penguins right winger Rick Tocchet said.

"Radiation — people don't realize what that stuff does to you. He was nothing short of brilliant, in my eyes."

Lemieux's teammates weren't the only ones impressed. This was an enormous victory for the Flyers, who are struggling to stay in playoff contention and had been 0-10-4 in their previous 14 games against the Penguins.

Philadelphia goalie Dominic Roussel halts Lemieux. Right, Lemieux and Kevin Stevens.

Still, Philadelphia coach Bill Dineen went out of his way to praise Lemieux for playing on the same day he completed his radiation therapy.

"Obviously, that's where his heart is, in playing hockey," Dineen said.

Lemieux said the radiation has robbed him of his sense of taste, but his play last night made it clear his hockey skills came through the therapy with no trouble.

It's no coincidence that the Penguins' power play, which had been ineffective for several weeks, converted three of five chances on the night he rejoined it. With Lemieux in charge, the Penguins moved the puck quickly and with confidence, and thus were able to consistently create scoring chances.

"He's just great on that right side (of the ice)," Tocchet said. "He just opens up so much more (ice). We get a lot more point shots, and Kevin Stevens gets free a little more."

Lemieux, his energy level sapped by the cumulative effects of the radiation, said he was "just a little tired at the end of the game," although that fatigue wasn't evident in his play.

Lemieux had looked somewhat tentative during his first few shifts, but his confidence returned after he had been on the ice a few times.

"Anytime you're out for two months or a long period of time, you don't know what to expect," he said. "That's what happened early in the game."

The Penguins actually would prefer to forget most of the first period. Ron Francis gave them a 1-0 lead with a power-play goal at 3:07, but Mark Recchi, Josef Beranek and Kevin Dineen beat Penguins goalie Tom Barrasso before the first intermission.

The Penguins rebounded with goals by Lemieux and Stevens in the first 3 1/2 minutes of the second period, and Dineen decided to replace goalie Dominic Roussel with Tommy Soderstrom. It was a move that probably saved the game for Philadelphia, because Soderstrom was brilliant the rest of the way.

Rod Brind'Amour put Philadelphia back in front, 4-3, at 5:33 of the second,

3.2.93

but Stevens pulled the Penguins even again at 13:57. There was no more scoring until 16:27 of the third, when Philadelphia defenseman Garry Galley beat Barrasso from above the left faceoff dot for the game-winner.

When Lemieux was diagnosed with Hodgkin's disease in mid-January, most of the Penguins said they would be happy if he made it back with a couple of weeks left in the regular season. Well, there's more than a month to go, and Lemieux looks like he's ready to get back into the grind.

"A lot of us thought it would be the end of March," Tocchet said. "Here it's early March and he's playing."

Mind you, Lemieux didn't have a normal workload last night. He took a regular shift and got extensive ice time on the power play, but was not used as a penalty-killer. Of course, the pregame plan had been to only use him when the Penguins had a man-advantage.

"What you saw tonight was one pretty amazing thing for a guy who wasn't supposed to play that much," Stevens said.

Even Lemieux, who judges his own work more harshly than any outsider, seemed fairly satisfied with what he did against the Flyers.

"I didn't have the jump I wanted tonight, but it's been a long two months," he said. "So slowly, I'll get back on top of my game."

But he reached a far more important pinnacle last night. He played hockey again, injected a little normalcy into a life that had been disrupted so severely less than two months ago.

Lemieux confronted the disease that threatened his life and, from all indications, beat it. Badly. He's always played to win, and it looks as if he's done it in a big way this time.

"If you don't have courage, you're not going to beat it," Lemieux said. "It's my nature to fight back."

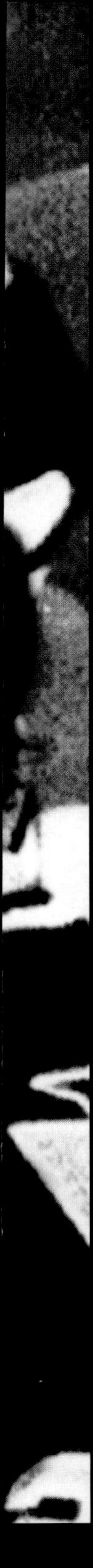

'ONE OF THE GUYS AGAIN'

By Dave Molinari
Pittsburgh Post-Gazette

PHILADELPHIA — When Mario Lemieux was diagnosed with Hodgkin's disease in mid-January, he assumed it would be a difficult trip back to the NHL.

He didn't discover how difficult until yesterday.

Lemieux's problem wasn't with complications from radiation treatments for his lymphatic system cancer. He had his 22nd — and final — session yesterday morning, and never experienced side effects more serious than minor fatigue and a dry throat.

But actually getting to Philadelphia, where Lemieux rejoined his teammates after being out since Jan. 5, turned out to be more difficult than anyone could have envisioned. Once there, Lemieux had a goal and an assist in the Penguins' 5-4 loss to the Flyers.

Lemieux was booked on a commercial flight from Pittsburgh International Airport to Philadelphia at 10 a.m. yesterday, but that plane got fogged in in Chicago.

After the fourth delay in the flight was announced, Lemieux called the Penguins office and asked the team to find a private plane to carry him across the state.

The Penguins did, and Lemieux and two members of the public-relations staff made a quick trip to Allegheny County Airport. They boarded a corporate jet there and arrived in Philadelphia at around 1 p.m.

The three then took a limousine to the team's hotel, and Lemieux did not surface until shortly before 5 p.m., when he appeared in the lobby.

He autographed a Penguins sweater thrust at him by a fan and had a brief exchange with a reporter, who jokingly told Lemieux he should worry about performing well in the postgame news conference, not the game.

He then was escorted to a cab by hotel security, who were assigned to shield Lemieux from the autograph-seekers waiting in front of the hotel.

When he arrived at the Spectrum, Lemieux was met by a throng of media on hand for his comeback. Newspapers from Toronto, New York, Washington and Boston sent reporters to the game.

Lemieux received a warm ovation from the sparse crowd in the Spectrum during the pregame skate, and the applause was louder when he was announced as a starter.

But the cheering didn't peak until Lemieux skated onto the ice before the game, and the usually hostile Spectrum crowd greeted him with a standing ovation that lasted about 90 seconds.

The Hodgkin's disease, and a bout of back pain that preceded it by about a week, forced Lemieux to miss 23 games. He has sat out 147 games because of various injuries during his eight-plus seasons in the NHL.

"We're used to Mario taking some time off, and then coming back," left winger Bob Errey said.

That doesn't mean the Penguins weren't excited about Lemieux's return.

"It will obviously give the team a boost, physically as well as mentally," defenseman Paul Stanton said. "It's going to make us feel good that Mario is a healthy person."

They feel so good about it, in fact, that Lemieux can expect to receive some serious abuse from his teammates in coming days. Lemieux stopped being a cancer patient and resumed being a pro hockey player last night, so any exemption he had from the verbal barbs that fly around the locker room has expired.

"He'll get treated just like he always did," right winger Joe Mullen said.

"I'm sure that's the only way Mario would want it, to just be one of the guys again."

EVEN PHILLY FANS CHEER FOR MARIO

BY GENE COLLIER
Pittsburgh Post-Gazette

HUNDREDS OF TICKETS REMAINED at midday yesterday for what appeared a seriously inconsequential hockey game between the defending Stanley Cup champions and the Flyers, now an NHL subspecies. But by the time Mario Lemieux rode a black-and-white taxi out of Society Hill and arrived in South Philadelphia about 5:15, the bespectacled blonde in the Flyers ticket office was losing her patience. ¶ "No sir, no sir, no sir," she squawked as evenly as possible into her headset. "Only a handful of single tickets remain and only at the ticket office. No sir, no sir, no sir."

Punch.

"Flyers ticket office. ... No sir, no sir, no sir."

She rolled her eyes.

Uh-oh.

In a city that once reveled in winning a players' poll as having the worst collection of fan rabble in the country, you had to wonder what herd of misanthropes was determined to fill up the building last night upon the compelling return of Lemieux, the game's ultimate warrior, on the rebound from the ultimate opponent.

"It would have been a lot nicer to start at home in Pittsburgh with all the fans and all the excitement," Lemieux said after as remarkably courageous a performance as he's authored in a career virtually crammed with them. "But the fans here in Philadelphia were great and that feels good, especially on the road."

Absolutely.

The nature of the gene pool for this audience is thoroughly documented.

Yes, they really did boo Santa. Yes, they booed the Easter Bunny, too.

The worst was Kiteman. Poor Kiteman was the ceremonial first-ball delivery man for several openers at Veterans Stadium. On wide plastic skis, he plummeted from the roof of the stadium down a ramp that would launch him from the upper deck, with varying degrees of success.

One year, at the climax of his approach, he slid off the runway and crashed into the first row of seats in the upper deck. A second later and he would not have averted, well, death. And ...

"BOOOOOO!"

BUT LAST NIGHT, PRECISELY seven weeks from the announcement that Lemieux had been diagnosed with Hodgkin's disease and had had a large malignant lymph node removed from his neck, Philadelphia found something not even it could boo.

Inside the Spectrum, America's showplace, the assemblage is not as incorrigibly hostile in that it has occasionally known fulfillment. Two Stanley Cups and an NBA championship have been won by its tenants over the years, and in a fantasy dimension, they'd witnessed a pretty courageous performance by a long-odds local pug named Rocky Balboa against that Creed guy.

The consequences for Rocky were merely a mangled story line. The consequences for Lemieux were potentially grave.

So at 7:31, with the announcement of the starting lineups, the name of Mario Lemieux was cheered enthusiastically, and when he appeared on the ice for the national anthem, a highly respectful 90-second ovation brought from him a raised stick and a wave.

All of it, gratifying as it was, was part of what Lemieux had wanted to put behind him, and his desire to do that was what drove him to come back so quickly.

"I felt good the last couple of weeks and I wasn't thinking much about the cancer," Lemieux said. "I wanted to come back earlier, but the doctors wouldn't let me."

It sounded late last night that Lemieux's view of his cancer was of something totally independent of his hockey mission. He wanted to put his singular skills back on the ice, and never really considered that he would not.

Though in the early minutes of last night's game it was evident he had missed two months. The goal he scored was not in itself impressive — he in fact sneaked a changeup past starting goalie Dominic Roussel and contributed to Roussel's early hook — but the way his incomparable offensive clairvoyance locked in so quickly surely was.

"Basically that was Lemieux," said Philadelphia coach Bill Dineen. "For a guy who's been out that long to come in and make the plays he did, it's incredible. You can't give him enough credit for the way he played. Coming off a treatment this morning, you can't give him enough credit. You can't give him enough credit just for showing up."

Now the night Lemieux wanted behind finally is, and he sustains himself on hockey gifts and medical advice.

"They just tell me to eat as much as I can," he said. "I've lost my taste. I can't taste anything; it all tastes the same. That's a side effect of the radiation."

He's lost that, and a bad lymph node, and nothing else.

Nothing.

Lemieux hops over the boards for his first shift since being diagnosed with Hodgkin's disease. He even beat Dominic Roussel for a goal.

Lemieux continues climb back with six-point night

Washington	**0**	**0**	**5**	**— 5**
Pittsburgh	**2**	**3**	**2**	**— 7**

By Dave Molinari
Pittsburgh Post-Gazette

Scotty Bowman says he wants to take it slowly to make certain he doesn't put too much of a strain on Mario Lemieux. How thoughtful. You can be sure the Washington Capitals appreciated Bowman's approach last night.

But I don't think they noticed.

Lemieux didn't get his normal quota of ice time in the Penguins' 7-5 victory at the Civic Arena, but the Capitals saw more than enough of Lemieux. Usually with his arms raised.

Lemieux had four goals and two assists to ring up his second most productive offensive game of the season, a performance surpassed only by his seven-point effort in a 9-4 victory against San Jose Dec. 5. Not bad for a guy still trying to shake the effects of treatments for Hodgkin's disease.

"He's getting better," Penguins defenseman Larry Murphy said. "He's feeling stronger. ... His hands are definitely there, that's for sure."

Lemieux returned to the lineup a little more than two weeks ago and still hasn't assumed his normal workload of 30-35 minutes a game.

"His timing is right there," said Bowman. "It's just a matter of not giving him too big an overload."

To that end, Bowman kept Lemieux off the penalty-killing unit.

Lemieux celebrates after his second of four goals.

3.18.93

"He didn't kill penalties tonight, which I think maybe helped him conserve a lot of his energy for the power play and even strength."

Lemieux said it is "hard to say" how close he is to being 100 percent, but made it clear he intends to challenge Buffalo Sabres center Pat LaFontaine for the NHL scoring championship. LaFontaine, who has played in 70 games, is first with 128 points; Lemieux, who has played in 46, has 118. "That's certainly my plan, to try to catch LaFontaine," Lemieux said. "It's going to be a good race."

The same should be true of the Penguins' battle with Montreal for the President's Trophy. They are tied with the Canadiens for first place in the overall standings.

The victory last night was the Penguins' 25th on home ice, tying a franchise record set in 1974-75 and matched in 1990-91. The Penguins (43-21-6) have won four consecutive games for the first time since Nov. 17-23 and lead the second-place Capitals by 17 points in the Patrick Division.

Lemieux set the tone early, firing a shot past goalie Don Beaupre one minute into the first period. "Every time I score on the first shift, it gets everybody going," Lemieux said.

Lemieux scored again at 4:28, and Lemieux and his linemates — Jaromir Jagr and Kevin Stevens — each got a goal in the second period.

"If you play scared of Lemieux's line, they're going to kill you," Capitals defenseman Al Iafrate said. "And that's what we did."

The Penguins gave the Capitals plenty to fear as they turned in some of their finest hockey of the season while running up a 5-0 lead in the first 40 minutes.

"When the game was on the line in the first two periods, we were doing things we hadn't done in a long time," Bowman said. "We were moving the puck very quickly out of our own zone."

Chances are they were inspired by a pregame meeting that featured a highlights tape from Game 4 of the Stanley Cup finals last spring. It underscored the importance of rapid puck movement, and the lesson wasn't lost on the Penguins.

Lemieux and Shawn McEachern beat Jim Hrivnak, who replaced Beaupre, in the third period, when Washington whittled the lead from 7-1 to 7-5.

But Coach Terry Murray wasn't impressed by his team's late comeback. "The horse was out of the barn and the barn door was closed."

The Capitals scored their final four goals against Ken Wregget, who replaced Tom Barrasso at 5:35 of the third period and had not played since Feb. 14. Barrasso, who stopped 25 of 26 shots, pulled himself from the game because of a swollen right knee, but said his injury is not severe.

The Penguins are not likely to rush him into the lineup before he is ready, considering their enormous lead in the Patrick Division. Much of that cushion can be traced to the 19-9-2 record inside the division.

Lemieux's deja vu: four more goals

Philadelphia	**0**	**0**	**3**	**— 3**
Pittsburgh	**2**	**5**	**2**	**— 9**

By Dave Molinari
Pittsburgh Post-Gazette

Philadelphia coach Bill Dineen knew Mario Lemieux could have a game like this.

Been there. Seen that.

Probably on a scouting tape this week. And certainly in his worst nightmares.

Lemieux added another chapter to his legend — and gave his team lots of footage for this season's highlight film — by ringing up four power-play goals and one assist in the Penguins' 9-3 victory against the Flyers at the Civic Arena. Forty-eight hours earlier, he had four goals and two assists in a 7-5 victory against Washington.

"It was the Lemieux show all over again," Dineen said. It's not clear if he realized the sequel was every bit as riveting as the original.

Lemieux's latest rampage moved him to within eight points of Buffalo center Pat LaFontaine in the NHL scoring race. What has to concern LaFontaine is that he got three points yesterday, but Lemieux still sliced his lead to 131-123.

"He (LaFontaine) is probably a little bit nervous right about now," Penguins left winger Kevin Stevens said. "If he can hang onto this lead, it's a credit to him, but I've still got my

Lemieux is all smiles because the game is all Pittsburgh — 9-3 over Philadelphia with four goals and two assists by the Penguins captain.

3.20.93

money on Mario to beat him. And I think he will."

The odds on that happening seemed a lot longer when Lemieux returned to the Penguins' lineup March 2 after being sidelined for nearly two months by Hodgkin's disease, but Lemieux has made a career of doing the improbable.

"You know when he has two months off, it's going to take him a little while to get it going," said Penguins center Ron Francis. "But I think he's started to figure out how to play the game again."

Uh, yeah. Seeing Lemieux put up 11 points in two games made it fairly clear he has regained a bit of his old feel for the game.

And remember, the Penguins still are trying to ease Lemieux back into his traditional role. He made a brief penalty-killing appearance last night, but still isn't getting quite his normal amount of playing time.

"We're trying to hold his ice time down, but a game like tonight, he had a chance to pick up some points," Coach Scotty Bowman said. "And he did."

Lemieux's outburst overshadowed superb nights by several of his teammates. Francis, for example, had a goal and four assists, but that could get him nothing more than the No. 2 star.

The victory was the Penguins' fifth in the row, a run surpassed only by a 7-0 streak Oct. 13-27, and raised their record to 44-21-6. Their magic numbers are 7 (a playoff berth) and 12 (the Patrick Division title).

It also was the Penguins' 26th win of the season on home ice, breaking a franchise record set in 1974-75 and matched in 1990-91.

For the Flyers, this defeat moved them closer to their inevitable elimination from the playoff race. They are 11 points out of fourth place.

"I don't think anybody quit," Dineen said. "But maybe we are a little in awe of them."

That would be understandable. The Penguins' offense, which had struggled for more than a month, has generated 16 goals in the past two games.

"It's been a lot of fun out there the last couple nights," Stevens said.

Last night, the fun started when Lemieux scored at 15:08 of the first period. Joe Mullen beat Tommy Soderstrom, Philadelphia's starting goalie, before the intermission, and the Penguins put the game out of reach with five goals during the second.

Lemieux (two), Rick Tocchet, Troy Loney and Francis got those goals, which were enough to convince Dineen to replace Soderstrom with Dominic Roussel for the final 20 minutes.

The Penguins moved through the neutral zone like a tsunami during the first two periods, as the Philadelphia defensemen threatened to set a land-speed record for backpedaling.

"When we get skating, we can score a lot of goals," Lemieux said.

They got more than they needed during the first two periods, but the Penguins again relaxed during the third. And for the second time in as many games, goalie Tom Barrasso lost his bid for a shutout during the final 20 minutes.

Josef Beranek, Eric Lindros and Rod Brind'Amour scored for Philadelphia before Jaromir Jagr and Lemieux closed out the scoring for the Penguins. "It seems like we're putting away teams in the first two periods, then kind of floating around in the third," Stevens said.

"Which is not a good habit to get into, but it doesn't really matter because come playoff time, we're going to play 60 minutes and the games aren't going to be 7-0."

Probably not, but if the Penguins continue to play as they have during the past few games, anything is possible. Their recent slump clearly is over, and they have focused on preparing for their run at a third straight Stanley Cup.

FOLLOW-UP

The Penguins' winning streak ended at 17, an NHL record. In the playoffs, they defeated New Jersey in the first round before losing to the New York Islanders.

Lemieux caps 32nd hat trick with 500th goal

Pittsburgh	2	1	4	— 7
NY Islanders	0	4	1	— 5

BY DAVE MOLINARI
Pittsburgh Post-Gazette

UNIONDALE, N.Y. — THE Penguins knew there would be some growing pains after they overhauled their lineup during the offseason.

Losing to the New York Islanders isn't easy, but the Penguins (3-2-1) made it look that way before salvaging a 7-5 victory at Nassau Coliseum.

They squandered a two-goal lead against the Islanders, who have come by their 1-6-1 record honestly, and likely would have lost if Mario Lemieux hadn't spearheaded a third-period comeback with some inspired work.

Lemieux capped his 32nd hat trick by getting the 500th goal of his career at 17:12 of the third period. That goal came in his 605th NHL game, faster than anyone in league history except Wayne Gretzky (575).

"The big guy turned it up a little bit," Penguins coach Eddie Johnston said.

"I was happy in the third with our effort."

Embarrassed as the Penguins had to be by much of their performance, at least it happened pretty much in private.

The game was played before a family-and-friends turnout of 8,384. That total didn't include New York Rangers defenseman Ulf Samuelsson, who is sidelined by a shoulder injury and dropped by to watch his former teammates.

If Samuelsson had been nursing any misgivings about being traded away from the Penguins, they likely passed before he headed home last night. The Penguins surely didn't look much like the team he won two Stanley Cups with.

The game began well enough for the Penguins as forward Bryan Smolinski, who didn't get a point in his first six games this season, needed less than two shifts to pick up an assist while playing left wing with Ron Francis and Jaromir Jagr.

Francis staked the Penguins to a 1-0 lead at 4:57 of the first period, tossing a rebound past goalie Tommy Soderstrom after a Smolinski shot had slammed off the left goal post. Jagr also received an assist on the goal, Francis' fourth of the season.

Smolinski nearly scored 30 seconds into the game when he had a chance to put a Jagr rebound into an empty net, but an Islander got a stick on his shot and the puck went over the glass.

Lemieux raised the Penguins' lead to 2-0 with a power-play goal at 18:04. He got the puck at the top of the right circle and drove a slap shot between Soderstrom's legs while Alexander Semak was serving a double-minor for spearing Penguins defenseman Francois Leroux.

The goal was Lemieux's fourth of the season; assists went to Norm Maciver and Jagr.

Lemieux's goal put the Penguins in position to take control of the game — especially when New York defenseman Mathieu Schneider had to leave with bruised ribs — but they let the Islanders get within a goal early in the second period.

Semak scored it at 1:24 by poking a loose puck between goalie Tom Barrasso's legs from near the left circle.

Markus Naslund nearly restored the Penguins' two-goal cushion at 8:50, when he picked his way through the New York defense, but his backhander hit the left post.

Lemieux got a penalty at 11:03 after he drove Islanders rookie Todd Bertuzzi into the boards from behind at 11:03, and New York used that man-advantage to tie the game.

Zigmund Palffy, one of the Islanders' few productive forwards,

500 CLUB

Mario Lemieux joined an elite group of players with his 500th goal. The leaders and Lemieux:

PLAYER	GOALS
1. Wayne Gretzky*	815
2. Gordie Howe	801
3. Marcel Dionne	731
4. Phil Esposito	717
5. Mike Gartner*	634
19. Mario Lemieux*	500

* *active*

10.26.95

Lemieux leaves the Islanders falling all over themselves. He scored his 500th NHL goal in the third period of the game.

The Penguins wasted little time making amends for that miserable second period, however, as Lemieux tied the game 19 seconds into the third. He broke behind the New York defense, took a perfect lead pass from Naslund and beat Soderstrom between the legs.

"That was a great play to send him in," Johnston said.

Lemieux played a pivotal role in the Penguins' go-ahead goal at 10:36, too. He won a faceoff in the New York zone cleanly to Sandstrom, who beat Soderstrom from the top of the left circle to give the Penguins a 5-4 lead.

Jagr added a critical goal at 12:03, swooping across the slot and flipping a backhander into the net during a power play to make it 6-4.

got the goal, beating Barrasso from inside the right circle at 12:42.

THE PENGUINS SURVIVED A roughing call against Smolinski at 14:47, but Palffy struck again at 17:01 to put New York in front. He carried the puck down the left side and, after drawing Barrasso out of the net, snapped in a shot from a sharp angle to make it 3-2.

That goal seemed to anger the Penguins, and they responded with one by Tomas Sandstrom at 18:18. He knocked in his seventh of the season after Soderstrom failed to control a chest-high shot by Dmitri Mironov.

Sandstrom's goal pulled the Penguins even, but not for long. Ten seconds after he scored, Travis Green steered a Bertuzzi pass behind Barrasso to put New York in front again.

His goal meant the Islanders, who had averaged two goals in their first seven games this season, scored four on the Penguins in 17 minutes, four seconds.

"We didn't play very well in the first two periods," Lemieux said.

Jagr's goal grew in importance at 14:47, when Wendel Clark got his first goal as an Islander. Clark, a non-factor since being acquired from Colorado on the eve of the season, swept in a backhander from the crease to make it a one-goal game.

New York, however, could get no closer and Lemieux scored again to assure the Penguins would slip into the night with a couple of points that might easily have been lost.

Lemieux has third five-goal game

St. Louis	**2**	**1**	**1**	**— 4**
Pittsburgh	**3**	**2**	**3**	**— 8**

BY DAVE MOLINARI
Pittsburgh Post-Gazette

HIS FIRST SON WAS BORN Sunday, and Mario Lemieux thought it would be nice to do something special to welcome his boy into the world.

Can't blame a fella for that.

It's kind of scary, though, to imagine what Lemieux might have pulled off if his wife had had twins.

As it was, he scored five goals and set up two others in the Penguins' 8-4 victory against Wayne Gretzky-led St. Louis at the Civic Arena. And while Lemieux, by his own admission, "could have had a couple more," it's unlikely young Austin Nicholas Lemieux will hold that against his daddy.

After all, Lemieux did come through with his 37th NHL hat trick, the third five-goal performance of his career, and his 800th assist. As individual efforts go, it was a keeper.

"It doesn't happen too often, to be able to do that," Lemieux said.

Lemieux's rampage helped the Penguins (44-25-4) to push their lead over the New York Rangers to four points in the Eastern Conference. It also took a lot of the intrigue away from the races to lead the NHL in goals and points.

Lemieux opened up spreads of four goals (63-59) and seven points (146-139) over teammate Jaromir Jagr, who got just one assist against St. Louis.

"Tonight, he was a little tired," Lemieux said, chuckling. "Maybe he needs a couple games off."

Jagr won't be taking any time off, but Blues forward Shayne Corson probably will. He got a concussion and broken jaw when Penguins defenseman Jean-Jacques Daigneault, not known as a big hitter, laid him out with a crushing check three minutes into the game.

"That was a big hit," Penguins center Petr Nedved said. A timely one, too, because the Penguins opened the scoring about a half-minute later.

Lemieux got the goal at 3:35, carrying the puck down the right side and fighting through a Chris Pronger hook before flipping a shot between goalie Grant Fuhr's legs.

"I was ready to play early," Lemieux said. "I felt very good."

Although the Penguins failed to convert on a five-on-three power play that ran 31 seconds midway through the period, Bryan Smolinski made it 2-0 during a power play at 11:32.

Smolinski punched in a loose puck from the right side of the crease for his 24th, a goal that prompted Blues coach Mike Keenan to replace Fuhr with Jon Casey.

Brett Hull cut the Penguins' lead to 2-1 at 13:02 by tipping a Pronger shot past goalie Ken Wregget for a power-play goal, and Stephane Matteau tied it on a harmless-looking shot from the left dot at 14:33.

But Blues defenseman Murray Baron short-circuited his team's momentum at 15:29, when he began to pummel Nedved for no apparent reason. The Penguins were awarded another power play, and Lemieux needed only eight seconds to capitalize.

He became the first player to hit the 60-goal plateau at 15:37, whipping the puck past Casey from outside the left hash.

The Penguins failed to capitalize on another two-man advantage in the second period, but three seconds after the first penalty expired, Lemieux completed his hat trick by throwing in a shot from inside the left circle at 8:43.

Lemieux didn't let up. The Penguins were killing a penalty a few minutes later when he picked off a Hull pass at the right point and broke in alone on Casey.

A few dekes later, Casey spread his pads and Lemieux snapped the puck between them at 11:15 for a short-handed goal, his league-leading seventh.

"He's a pretty scary player when he gets going," Nedved said. "There's nobody out there who's going to stop him."

AT THAT POINT, LEMIEUX'S thoughts drifted toward the NHL record for goals in a game, seven.

The sixth goal never came, however, and for a while, it looked as if the Penguins' two points might not, either.

Their lead began to evaporate when Pronger steered a Christer Olsson pass by Wregget for a power-play goal at 12:05, and Rob Pearson punched in a loose puck at 3:05 of the third to get the Blues within one at 5-4.

But Lemieux — who else? — gave

3.26.96

Lemieux calls for the puck against the Blues; his teammates were wise to oblige.

the Penguins a bit of breathing room by knocking a Ron Francis pass behind Casey for his 63rd goal at 6:08, eight seconds after the Penguins killed off a penalty.

Lemieux, who got even more ovations than points, earned assist No. 800 at 11:35, when Brad Lauer swatted in a loose puck to put the Penguins up, 7-4.

Lemieux finally saw the Penguins get a goal in which he didn't play a part at 16:04, when Nedved got his 40th on a wrist shot from the slot to close out the scoring.

By then, Lemieux already had scored seven points and made a critical one: With his family crisis behind him, he is ready to raise his game back to its usual dizzying level.

"It's been very difficult for myself and my family the last couple of months," he said. "By the way I was playing, I think everybody knew something was up. I was not able to play very well. I think my head was somewhere else."

But even though his son, who was born several months prematurely, and wife Nathalie have plenty of recovering to do in coming weeks, Lemieux believes he's going to be able to concentrate on his job for the first time in a while.

"The baby's doing great, and my wife's doing great," Lemieux said. "So I can go back and think about hockey now and do my job."

LEMIEUX VS. GRETZKY: NO COMPARISON

BY GENE COLLIER
Pittsburgh Post-Gazette

THAT WAS A STANDING ROOM ONLY CROWD cramming the Civic Arena, with little explanation for it necessary beyond the presence of the globe's two greatest hockey artists, Mario Lemieux, and, of course, Jaromir Jagr. ¶ But then, Lemieux and Jagr paint masterpieces here regularly, a condition that, while roundly appreciated, generally leaves a couple hundred seats empty. So the little bump Howard Baldwin's ledger got from last night might have been attributable to the opposition, namely the St. Louis Blues and newly acquired center/legend, the one, the only, Craig MacTavish.

Additionally, what's left of Wayne Gretzky was in the building, and while many thought this to be of significance in some time-warped juxtaposition to the still incomparable Lemieux, any significance certainly wasn't evident.

Lemieux scored five goals, a cadenza unequaled anywhere in the NHL this season, and Jagr seemed to defer to Lemieux's greatness as if to allow a clearer comparison to Gretzky. As if the fact that Lemieux has scored three goals for every one scored by Gretzky this season while playing in 13 fewer games allows any heated analysis.

"I think when you play with his ability and his intelligence," said Gretzky of Lemieux, "maybe he doesn't do some of the things he did in the past, but he's come to compensate for some things he's lost and he still gets the job done.

"He had a tremendous game. If it weren't for our goalies, he probably would have had six or seven goals."

Gretzky, obviously, plays with intelligence, too, and probably more than with ability. He's known and played the compensation game, which, like the real game, gets harder with every disposed calendar.

Thus this whole premise is as unfair to Gretzky as it is to 66. At age 35, Gretzky's got 10 Art Ross trophies, nine Harts, five Lester B. Pearsons, four Lady Byngs, two Conn Smythes, four Stanley Cups and a partridge in a

fair tree of 61 NHL records. He's also at the stage of a career where you can have him for draft picks and Craig Johnson if you throw in a couple of guys named Patrice and Roman, which is what free-lance genius Mike Keenan did Feb. 27.

Keenan, the coach and general manager, takes the same approach as a bridge painter. He finishes painting one end of the roster and starts back the other way, the only difference being that the current Blues roster is older than most of your major North American suspension bridges.

It isn't clear where the Blues feel they're headed in the postseason with so many players you thought were dead, but nowhere would be a good guess so long as they take the frequency of stupid penalties they have all year.

"WE SEEM TO BE a very undisciplined team right now," said Gretzky. "We can't continue to take penalties that put us behind the 8-ball. You can't take holding penalties that have nothing to do with the game situation."

If you could buy a Stanley Cup, the big hardware would be on its way to St. Louis right now, but for all of Keenan's spending (and all the spending necessary to sneak Keenan away from the New York Rangers in 1994), the Blues are still a club as likely to lose as win.

Whether that says more about Gretzky at this stage or about Keenan is anybody's guess.

"Gretzky and Lemieux improve their hockey clubs immensely," Keenan said. "Tonight, Wayne just didn't have the people working with him. I'm sure if you ask Mario about his night he'll be very complimentary of the people around him. As great as these players might be, they can't do it without support people. Mario's support people were great."

For the record, Gretzky picked up an assist to avoid what would have been his first scoreless night going head-to-head with Lemieux. The two have been on the same pond 21 times, with Gretzky scoring 51 points and Lemieux 37. Pittsburgh's records against Gretzky's Oilers, Kings and Blues is 7-13-1, which might illuminate the difference more accurately.

There are worse things to be at 35 than a nice little player who can pump up a club desperately in need of offense, but right now it's far more glorious to be the recurring miracle that is Mario Lemieux.

GAMES WE WON'T FORGET

Lemieux passes Penguins past Capitals

Pittsburgh	**2**	**2**	**0**	**— 4**
Washington	**0**	**0**	**1**	**— 1**

By Dave Molinari
Pittsburgh Post-Gazette

LANDOVER, MD. — THE PENguins broke out their third uniforms, and perhaps that was an act of desperation. Which doesn't mean it was a bad idea.

After all, the Penguins needed a victory, and had been 6-0 during the regular season when wearing those unusual duds. Besides, even if that streak were broken, they could make a nice fashion statement as they hurtled toward the offseason.

But the arrival of summer has been pushed back for at least a few more days, and it's not because the Penguins left their normal road uniforms at home.

Their 4-1 victory against Washington at USAir Arena was a matter of style, all right, but it had nothing to do with their wardrobe.

It was about attitude. About playing hard. About working in both ends of the rink, and fighting along the boards and in the corners like they cared.

And it was about Mario Lemieux.

It was quite a change from their sloppy, inconsistent performances in Games 1 and 2 of this first-round playoff series. And why they were able to hold a 2-0 lead for the first time in three games.

There was another change that had an impact on the outcome, too: Washington coach Jim Schoenfeld's decision to replace goalie Olaf Kolzig with Jim Carey.

The captain shouts instructions to teammates during the Penguins' victory.

Kolzig had won Games 1 and 2 and is 3-0 against the Penguins in the playoffs, but Schoenfeld opted for Carey, who was pulled from Game 1 after allowing four goals on 16 shots.

Carey made some big-league stops last night, but the Penguins didn't seem bothered that he was back.

The Penguins won even though Lemieux and Jaromir Jagr were held

4.22.96

without a goal. Lemieux did his share, though, assisting on all four of the Penguins' goals.

Washington still has the upper hand in this series, holding a 2-1 lead going into Game 4 tomorrow at USAir Arena.

Winning Game 3 does, however, have at least two payoffs for the Penguins: It assures they will not be swept — an almost unthinkable embarrassment, given Washington's watered-down lineup; and guarantees there will be a Game 5 Friday at the Civic Arena.

That should please the corporate accountants, who had to be cringing at the thought of having only two playoff dates.

About the only ominous development for the Penguins was a possible injury to Jagr. He went to the locker room midway through the third period after absorbing a hard hit from Washington's Mark Tinordi, and there was no immediate word on whether he went off as a precaution or because he had been hurt.

Washington ran up a 10-3 advantage in shots during the opening period — including the first seven of the game — but the Penguins got the only two goals of the first 20 minutes. And they nearly put in a couple more.

Their first good scoring chance came at 5:55, when an apparent short-handed breakaway by Lemieux was halted by a solid open-ice hit. From referee Bill McCreary.

The Penguins were predictably displeased by that turn of events — they figured getting ahead last night was critical — but they benefited from an eerily similar play later in the game.

Ron Francis threw the Penguins' first shot of the game past Carey during a power play at 8:29, when he took a cross-ice feed from Lemieux and scored from the inner edge of the right circle.

Washington's Joe Juneau came within millimeters of tying the game at 10:20, when his shot from the left circle rattled off the crossbar behind goalie Tom Barrasso, but the rest of the good chances in the period belonged to the Penguins.

Francis put a shot off the crossbar while short-handed at 14:39, and Capitals defenseman Jim Johnson had to give up his body — again — to spoil a good chance for Jagr later in that penalty. Jagr had a two-on-one break with Petr Nedved.

The Penguins finally came up with that elusive second goal at 17:52, as Glen Murray got his stick on a soft Sergei Zubov wrist shot from the right point to deflect it past Carey.

The Penguins had numerous chances to put the game out of reach early in the second period, but couldn't capitalize on their opportunities.

Carey stopped a Kevin Miller shot with the shaft of his stick two minutes into the period, and 75 seconds later Murray took a pass from Lemieux and slammed a shot off the right post.

Then, as the middle of the period approached, Carey seemed to find the form that has made of him on the NHL's premier goalies.

He made a series of excellent stops, including several on Nedved, and the Capitals seemed to be gearing up to make a run at the Penguins. But the unfortunate positioning of an official — the same thing that cost the Penguins a potential goal early in the game — helped to make the Penguins' third goal possible.

As the Penguins carried the puck through the neutral zone, Washington defenseman Steve Poapst backed into linesman Dan Schachte, turning a nondescript rush into a two-on-one break.

With Poapst out of the play, Murray carried the puck unimpeded down the right side. He then slipped the puck across to Dave Roche, who knocked it behind Carey for his first career playoff goal at 12:33.

The Capitals were particularly irate after the goal because McCreary had not called an apparent penalty against the Penguins in their defensive zone seconds before the play that made it 3-0.

If Roche's goal didn't deflate the Capitals, the one Kevin Miller scored four minutes before the second intermission surely did.

The play began when Lemieux knocked a Jim Johnson pass out of the air, then pushed the puck to Miller in the slot. Miller tossed a turning shot past Carey for his first of the series at 16:00 to give the Penguins their first four-goal lead of the series.

PENGUINS FINALLY SHOW LIFE

By Gene Collier
Pittsburgh Post-Gazette

LANDOVER, MD. — The NHL welcomed the Pittsburgh Penguins to the postseason with festive, moving ceremonies inside USAir Arena, ending speculation that the Washington Capitals would advance in the playoffs without their first-round opponent ever showing up. ¶ The Penguins, who won more games than any team in the conference in the regular season and had three of the league's top four scorers, were delayed in reaching playoff viability by hour after hour after hour of defensive indifference.

But on a night when perhaps not even defensive indifference could have overturned the four-goal lead the Penguins carved out of a typically desperate Washington team, this series lurched back toward equilibrium with a 4-1 Pittsburgh victory that had all the earmarks of actual work.

"We played a lot smarter when we got the lead today," said Penguins coach Eddie Johnston. "We stayed focused on what we were doing. We finished our checks. We were letting them off the hook a little in the first two games."

A little? The prospect of having its most opulent nest of marquee talent go up in flames even before the Stanley Cup playoffs assumed their own momentum was not a particularly favorable prospect for the league, which played an unwitting role in last night's episode on several fronts.

First, the league let the Penguins wear their jammies, the ultra-spiffy "third jersey" with the baby blue shoulder stripes and the cuddly Venetian blind motif on the back and breast.

Such an initiative requires league approval (how could I make that up?), and seeing as how the club was 6-0 in their jammies during the regular season, their addition for Game 3 of this struggle stood as the boldest strategical stroke by a Johnston-coached club in at least a week.

"We talked about wearing 'em," said Mario Lemieux. "It was (equipment manager) Steve Latin's idea." Of course, not everyone with the league appeared to be on the same page last night.

Referee Bill McCreary, for example, did not seem to have the agenda for a return to Penguins prowess when he personally halted a Lemieux breakaway with the game still scoreless. Lemieux, still looking for his first goal of the series, picked off a Washington pass in the neutral zone and whirled to bust into the Capitals' end, but McCreary was too quick for 66. Well, too clumsy, if you have to be technical about it.

McCreary took the body, even separating Lemieux from the puck. Lemieux stood erect in disgust. You can't blame him.

It's bad enough the league's officials won't enforce the new rules against the so-called neutral zone trap; it's worse when the referee goes so far as to execute it himself.

"He's a good defensive referee," Lemieux chuckled. "Yeah, he stood me up pretty good." Fortunately for Pittsburgh, a classic makeup call led to the third Penguins goal. By then, maybe the Capitals had begun to suspect something.

Glen Murray steamed out of the Penguins' end with Capitals defenseman Steve Poapst in effective pursuit but, again in the neutral zone, linesman Dan Schachte screened Poapst off the play, creating the kind of two-on-one the Penguins so infrequently managed by themselves in Games 1 and 2.

Murray flew down the right wing and feathered a pretty centering pass to Dave Roche, who beat surprise starter Jim Carey and gave life to the notion that the Penguins meant to play an entire game.

When that became certifiably evident, Washington coach Jim Schoenfeld succumbed to some cynical tactics, such as sending Kevin (Killer) Kaminski out on the power play, which is like sending a piano mover to tune a Steinway.

Penguins defenseman Neil Wilkinson, obviously incensed at this misapplication, took the opportunity afforded by a stoppage in front of the net to bludgeon Kaminski to the ice, which did not impress McCreary, who spent a very confused evening.

When Schoenfeld complained bitterly to the referee, McCreary called a bench minor against Washington. Kaminski served it. But McCreary evened that within seconds by calling Ron Francis (not your typical thug, exactly) for holding.

Things got out of hand in Game 3 early and stayed that way. The fact that they got that way on Pittsburgh's terms looked as much like happenstance as any Penguins revolution.

"We've still got to play a lot better," Johnston said, "if we expect to get another win here."

FOLLOW-UP

The Penguins won the series against the Capitals, four games to two, and advanced to the conference semifinals and finals. After defeating the New York Rangers in five games, the Penguins lost to the Florida Panthers in a seven-game series.

GAMES WE WON'T FORGET

Lemieux only the seventh to reach 600 goals

Vancouver	**2**	**1**	**1**	**— 4**
Pittsburgh	**2**	**2**	**2**	**— 6**

2.4.97

Teammates mob Lemieux after his milestone achievement during the third period.

BY DAVE MOLINARI
Pittsburgh Post-Gazette

IT WASN'T THE MOST SPECTACULAR goal Mario Lemieux has scored since he entered the NHL in 1984.

Or the most significant.

But when Lemieux threw the puck into an empty net from the left-wing boards with 55.2 seconds to play in the Penguins' 6-4 victory against Vancouver at the Civic Arena, he had picked up one of the most memorable goals of his career.

It was his 600th, making him only the seventh player in league history to get that many, and inspired an extended salute from the standing-room crowd of 17,355.

"I'm glad to get it here tonight," Lemieux said. "Having it happen in front of these fans is something I'll remember for a while."

Putting Lemieux's achievement in historical perspective doesn't take much. A glance at the other half-dozen players who have gotten 600 make the point quite nicely.

They are: Wayne Gretzky, Gordie Howe, Marcel Dionne, Phil Esposito, Mike Gartner and Bobby Hull.

"It's a pretty special list," Lemieux said. "To be included on that list is something I'll be able to cherish the rest of my life."

It's not something the fans who witnessed it are likely to forget anytime soon, either.

"It's kind of special that he got it here at home," Penguins coach Eddie Johnston said.

Lemieux did not accompany the Penguins to Montreal after the game because of tightness in his back. Although he will not be in the lineup when the Penguins meet the Canadiens tomorrow at the Molson Centre, team officials said he is expected to play when Detroit visits

the Civic Arena Saturday.

"It didn't feel too good tonight," Lemieux said. "I'm trying to get it under control."

Lemieux's goal clinched a victory that was very much in doubt with 2:06 to play in regulation, when Jyrki Lumme of Vancouver scored a goal that appeared to tie the game, 5-5.

Replay official Dale Ruth, however, ruled that Canucks forward Trevor Linden was in the crease before the puck, and referee Kerry Fraser disallowed the goal.

The Penguins, who lost goals in recent weeks when Jaromir Jagr and Jason Woolley were deemed to be in the crease, insisted replays left little room for interpretation. Or doubt.

"If you look at the film, there's no doubt about what happened," Johnston said. "Finally, it worked in our favor. It was an easy call, because he was there."

"As soon as we saw the replay, we knew it wasn't going to be a goal," center Petr Nedved said. "It's fair to us that it wasn't a goal."

The frenetic ending, with one goal disallowed and a historic one scored, was a fitting way to complete a game almost devoid of defense. Lapses and breakdowns were surpassed only by the number of quality scoring chances each team enjoyed.

"This reminds me of when I was playing out on the pond," Woolley said.

Not that anyone should be surprised the Penguins and Canucks would engage in a shootout. Both teams are comfortable in wide-open games.

"They have a tendency to play like that," Nedved said. "They like to play open hockey, and we like to play that, so it was almost whoever was going to have the last shot was going to win the game."

Suffice to say, neither coach was enamored of the style. Purists don't care much for such an offense-oriented game.

"Coaches don't," Nedved said. "Players do."

Penguins right winger Joe Mullen noted that, "once you're on the ice, the coaches can't do a lot," although Johnston said he had expressed concerns about it before the opening faceoff.

"You get afraid of games like this," Johnston said. "We talked about that. Because they lost a couple in a row, we think we're going to jump on a club like that and score a lot of goals."

Actually, the Penguins did just that, although they barely got enough to win.

Stu Barnes opened the scoring with a power-play goal at 6:23 of the first period. After Lumme countered for Vancouver at 8:28, Joe Dziedzic put the Penguins back in front at 13:20. Precisely 26 seconds later, Mike Sillinger pulled the Canucks even again.

Jaromir Jagr (11:52) and Mullen (12:04) scored 12 seconds apart in the second period to put the Penguins up two, but David Roberts beat goalie Patrick Lalime at 12:58 to get the Canucks back within one.

Sillinger tied the game with a short-handed goal at 1:57 of the third, but Ron Francis exploited — what else? — a defensive breakdown to ring up the game-winner at 11:28.

He was in the slot and, after taking a feed from Jagr, was able to skate unimpeded to the net and throw a backhander past Canucks goalie Kirk McLean for his 20th of the season. At that point, all that remained was for Lemieux to send the crowd home happy by scoring, which he did in the final minute.

Of course, that was nearly three hours after his first great opportunity of the evening. The game was only about 5 1/2 minutes old when Francis set him up at the left side of the Vancouver net, but Lemieux's stick shattered when he tried to shoot.

"I think he would have taken that one right off the bat, because it was such a great play," Johnston said. "He had the whole net, wide open, and his stick broke."

That wasn't the first good scoring chance of the game, and it certainly would not be the last. The game that unfolded was a classic shootout, and the Penguins managed to dodge enough bullets to survive.

"We like that kind of game," Mullen said. "We feel we can win those games. We just have to continue playing hockey the way we're capable."

Even if it's not necessarily the way the coach likes it.

"Having it happen in front of these fans is something I'll remember."

MARIO LEMIEUX

IS THIS THE 11TH HOUR FOR MARIO?

BY GENE COLLIER
Pittsburgh Post-Gazette

THERE WAS WITHOUT QUESTION AN AUGmented electricity in the Civic Arena ambiance for this episode. Calling it a charged atmosphere, however, would be reckless when you consider the typical decibels for a Penguins game approximate those of a wine-and-cheese reception at the library. ¶ It was way louder than that, and when you get 17,355 or more in the building anticipating the landmark 71st career goal of Vancouver Canucks defenseman Jyrki Lumme, you're gonna have juice; that's just one of the great axioms of sports.

And Jyrki Lumme, ladies and gentleman, didn't disappoint.

He pulled that big 66 kid to the ice in the first period and then pumped in a tying goal on a night when the Penguins actually appeared more concerned with trivia than with conceptual hockey, specifically the concept of protecting the puck.

Mario Lemieux needed one goal to make it 600 for his player-of-the-game, week, month, year, decade, century, and millennium career, and his teammates looked excessively determined to make it happen for him on home ice, as though having it wait until tonight in his hometown of Montreal or until the weekend in this same building would somehow devalue it.

"We pressed like hell," marveled Penguins coach Eddie Johnston. "You want to get something like this over with at home, so this was great."

He's a hopeless romantic.

But make it happen for him they did.

Ron Francis slid the puck to the left edge of the Vancouver blue line as 66 steamed toward an empty Canuck net with a 5-4 lead in the final minute. Lemieux accepted it, took a look at the net and a look at Lumme, the only Canuck defender back, and wristed No. 600 as perfectly as you'd anticipate into an open cage and into history.

The crowd snapped to attention, reigning chants and thanks, and his teammates watched a brief highlight package on the big scoreboard near the ceiling. Lemieux smiled through it

Lemieux salutes the Civic Arena crowd following the 600th goal of his spectacular NHL career.

without a hint of false modesty.

"To get a standing ovation in a game like this is something special," Lemieux said after some treatment for tightness in his famously cranky back. "I'm just glad it all happened here."

Nothing involving the attendant trivia of these final months of Lemieux's singularly brilliant nova on the vast and battered sports galaxy is going to alter Mario's enduring status as the most dominant athlete ever to compete for a Pittsburgh team, and by that I mean, yes, including Stan Terlecki.

Just so there's no confusion.

But the Penguins continue to play to roughly 96 percent of capacity, meaning that the populace is passing on opportunities to see Lemieux even as he's made just about every noise possible to indicate this is his final year.

If there are but 16 Civic Arena home dates and a highly indefinite number of home playoff games left in the hockey lifetime of Mario Lemieux, even this minimum of empty seats looks like an unflattering curiosity.

The number of people who'll say they were there last night will far exceed that 17,355 figure, but the number of people who will fully appreciate all the final numerology of this career isn't far greater than that. To understand the meaning of these numbers, wherever they end, — 620 goals, 890 assists, whatever — you have to get a grip on what they could have been. You have to have been in Pittsburgh.

"He might have had (an unprecedented) 900 goals," Johnston was saying in a good attempt at perspective.

"The last seven, eight years, he hasn't been able to play all the time. My first year (back) here, he couldn't tie his skates. He missed time with the Hodgkin's; he took a year off. There's no telling how many goals he could have scored.

"This is the first time in a long time he can play most of the games. I've seen him have more jump this year than he's had in a long time."

Of course, the words weren't out of the coach's mouth when news came that Lemieux will not make the trip to Montreal, hoping to have his back pain under control by the weekend.

And still, Lemieux's incredible level of play and relative youth (he's 31) tease the unvanquished question. Are these not the final months, not the final cadenza of it all?

"I don't think he's totally, in fact, made up his mind that he's not going to play again," Johnston said.

Lemieux moves ito sixth on goal-scoring list

Florida	0	2	1	— 3
Pittsburgh	2	2	0	— 4

By Dave Molinari
Pittsburgh Post-Gazette

The Penguins make no secret of their desire to move up in the Eastern Conference standings. Even if their reward for doing so turns out to be a best-of-seven slam dance with Florida, perhaps the most tenacious and relentless team in the NHL.

The same Florida that upset the Penguins in the Eastern Conference final last spring. The same Florida they beat, 4-3, at the Civic Arena, after fending off a predictably spirited comeback by the Panthers.

A playoff series with the Panthers might not seem like a very nice payoff for finishing the season strong, but it appears to be the best the Penguins can hope for at this point.

"There are no prizes in this conference," Penguins coach Craig Patrick said. "But we've got to continue playing well and, whatever draw we get, we get."

Florida coach Doug MacLean, meanwhile, did nothing to conceal his desire for a first-round matchup against the Penguins.

"I think it's going to be a great series," MacLean said. "I hope we play them. It would be fun."

The Penguins` victory last night was punctuated by another statistical milestone for center Mario Lemieux: His game-winner was the 610th goal of his career, tying him with Bobby Hull for sixth place on the NHL's all-time list.

The victory was the Penguins' second in a row and pulled them even with the New York Rangers for fifth place in the Eastern Conference. Both teams have 79 points and the Penguins hold a 36-35 advantage in victories, the first tiebreaker.

The entire Florida Panthers team gathered around Lemieux following the game to wish him well in his retirement.

The Penguins and New York have six games remaining and trail the fourth-place Panthers by five points. Florida has five games left, including its regular-season finale against the Penguins.

If the Panthers can hold onto the No. 4 spot, they will have home-ice advantage against the fifth seed during the first round. The team that finishes sixth in the conference will open the playoffs against the Atlantic Division runnerup, Philadelphia or New Jersey.

Bottom line: Regardless of who finishes where in the conference, no team

3.31.97

will make it to the second round without some scars.

"No matter who you play, it's going to be a battle," Penguins winger Garry Valk said.

True enough, and it was quite a skirmish the Penguins and Panthers staged . The Penguins ran up a big lead and Florida, as gritty and resilient as ever, came back strong enough to keep the outcome in doubt until the final seconds.

"That was a gratifying win," Patrick said. "We got off to a good start, and held on pretty well."

It helped that the Lemieux-Ron Francis-Jaromir Jagr line had two goals and four assists in its second game since Jagr's return from a groin injury.

"It makes it easier for everybody," Valk said. "Every team has a big line, and they're going to do the bulk of the scoring."

But it was Ian Moran who opened the scoring last night, deflecting a Kevin Hatcher shot between the legs of Florida goalie John Vanbiesbrouck at 6:21 of the first period. At 8:04, the lead became 2-0 when Josef Beranek was credited with deflecting a Darius Kasparaitis shot behind Vanbiesbrouck, although some replays suggested the puck actually struck Florida defenseman Robert Svehla.

Most importantly, the Penguins were going hard to the Panthers' net, and being rewarded for it. Florida, conversely, was limited to just eight shots on Penguins goalie Ken Wregget during the first 20 minutes.

"We drove to their net well, and didn't give up a whole lot of opportunities," Wregget said. "That's what we have to learn to do for 60 minutes."

The Penguins expanded their comfort zone at 3:04 of the second period, when Jagr pounced on a Lemieux rebound and flipped it into the open side of the net to make it 3-0. More than a few teams would fold after falling behind by a field goal on the road, but the Panthers don't make a habit of accepting defeat without a struggle.

"I don't think you ever have an easy game against Florida," Patrick said. "They work so hard, and when they get down, I don't know how they can work harder, but they seem to."

Scott Mellanby jammed a shot between Wregget's pads at 5:03 and defenseman Ed Jovanovski backhanded in a rebound at 14:33 to cut the Penguins' advantage to 3-2.

Florida's comeback was tribute to its tenacity and, to some degree, by a letdown on the Penguins' part.

Lemieux got what proved to be the decisive goal at 18:30 of the second, beating Vanbiesbrouck from the left hash after taking a cross-ice feed from Francis, but Florida didn't let up. Rob Niedermayer tossed a backhander behind Wregget at 7:36 of the third, but that was the final goal Florida could manufacture.

Not, of course, because of a lack of effort.

"I thought we played great in the second and third period," MacLean said. "We dominated them."

That's a bit of an overstatement, but hyperbole isn't the issue. And to hear the Penguins tell it, playoff matchups aren't a major concern just yet, either.

"I don't think it really matters who you play," Wregget said. "They're all good teams in there right now. The big thing is for us to play as well as we can for the remaining games and build on that, get some confidence going into the playoffs."

4.5.97

LEMIEUX, AT TOP OF HIS GAME, SAYS THIS YEAR WILL BE HIS LAST

WILL STAY IN CITY

HE THANKS HIS FANS

ACHIEVED HIS GOALS

TIMING WAS SURPRISE

“*This is the place I’m going to live the rest of my life.*”

MARIO LEMIEUX

By Shelly Anderson
Pittsburgh Post-Gazette

MARIO LEMIEUX MADE IT OFFICIAL, and he got to tell hundreds of his fans directly. ¶ The Penguins' superstar center confirmed during the Post-Gazette's 61st annual Dapper Dan Dinner at the Pittsburgh Hilton & Towers that this is his final NHL season. ¶ "I just wanted to take a couple of seconds to say that this will be my last year officially," Lemieux said after accepting a special Merci Mario award. ¶ He will be leaving hockey, but not Pittsburgh, his adopted home. ¶ "This is the place I'm going to live the rest of my life," said Lemieux, eliciting a roar of approval. ¶ Lemieux, 31, who led the Penguins to Stanley Cup championships in 1991 and 1992 and battled through back surgery and cancer, caught everyone — including club officials — off guard with the timing off his retirement announcement. ¶ "Even as of this afternoon, there were no plans for him to speak," said Tom McMillan, the Penguins vice president of communications.

The announcement itself, though, was not a surprise. Lemieux had said since last summer that he expected to retire after the 1997 playoffs.

"He's obviously indicated that over time and we had expected an announcement, but we thought it would be after the season," said Penguins President Donn Patton, who attended the dinner.

Afterward, Patton left a phone message for team owner Howard Baldwin, in case he was unaware.

The harder part, Patton said, is accepting the news.

"That's what I think a lot of people are going to have to come to grips with: Their chance to see the most talented hockey player in the world is coming to a close," he said.

The Penguins' regular season ends next Sunday at Boston. Their final home game before the playoffs is Tuesday night, also against Boston.

Lemieux is leading the league with 117 points on 49 goals and 68 assists. He has won the NHL scoring title (the Art Ross Trophy) five times.

Among his other NHL highlights: the Calder Trophy for rookie of the year in 1985, the Hart Trophy for league MVP three times, the Conn Smythe Trophy for playoff MVP twice, and a first-team All-Star four times.

Lemieux said in his 13 seasons with the Penguins he most wanted to help the team develop a winning tradition, and that he feels he did that.

The Penguins finished with the worst record in the league in 1983-84, thereby earning the first pick in the 1984 draft.

Eddie Johnston, then the Penguins' general manager and now assistant GM, got incredible trade offers from other teams for that draft pick, but he rejected them all and brought Lemieux to Pittsburgh. Some have credited Lemieux with saving the Penguins franchise.

Lemieux, who earlier in the day scored his 612th career goal, a shorthanded tally, in a 5-2 victory over Ottawa, said after his announcement that no one should be surprised.

"I think it's been well-publicized," he said. "I've said it all along."

Lemieux, who was Dapper Dan Sportsman of the Year for 1986 and 1988, was a finalist last night. Olympic gold medal wrestler Kurt Angle was honored for 1996.

Asked why he made it official last night, Lemieux shrugged.

"Might as well."

LEMIE

GAMES WE WON'T FORGET

Lemieux's a winner in final regular-season game

Boston	**0**	**0**	**1**	**—**	**1**
Pittsburgh	**1**	**1**	**1**	**—**	**3**

4.9.97

By Dave Molinari
Pittsburgh Post-Gazette

PATRICK LALIME NEVER CLAIMED that it was his night.

He insisted that the evening belonged to Mario Lemieux, who was making his final regular-season appearance at the Civic Arena.

And Lalime had a valid point, considering all that Lemieux has given to the Penguins since 1984.

But like it or not, Lalime ended up sharing the spotlight with Lemieux after the Penguins' 3-1 victory against Boston. It's kind of tough for a guy to hide after he stops 38 of 39 shots.

"He looked sharp," Penguins coach Craig Patrick said. "He had a good game."

Actually, Lemieux didn't have a bad one himself. He finished with a game-high 11 shots, even though he didn't earn a point until he assisted on Ed Olczyk's empty-net goal with 58 seconds left in regulation.

"Mario played a great game, even if he didn't score," Lalime said. "He had a ton of chances. He's still the best player. That was his show tonight."

Lemieux's assist stretched his scoring streak to six games, and he will become the first player to end his career averaging at least two points per game.

More importantly, the victory ran the Penguins' unbeaten streak to 4-0-1 and sustained their drive to move up in the Eastern Conference standings.

The victory clinched a seventh consecutive winning season for the Penguins (38-33-8) and lifted them into a tie with the New York Rangers for fifth place in the conference. They have a game in hand on New York and Florida, which is one point ahead of the Penguins and Rangers.

The Penguins, who finished with a home record of 25-11-5, will close out the season with three road games.

They will visit Tampa Bay, Florida and Boston.

The two points they took from the Bruins last night clearly were critical, but they might turn out to be costly, too. Wingers Jaromir Jagr and Josef Beranek left the game early because of sore groins, and there was no immediate word on how badly either is injured.

"At this point, I don't know," Patrick said. "We'll see how they are. With both of them, we just wanted to get them out for precautionary reasons."

Jagr went to the locker room late in the second period and did not return for the third. He did not speak to reporters immediately after the game, but appeared to be walking without any particular problem.

Jagr even took time to joke that 'I'm done," as he headed toward the team offices about 20 minutes after the game ended.

Lalime, filling in for Ken Wregget, said he was pleased with his play, that, "it's good to have a performance like that." It also was absolutely necessary because of the excellent work produced by his Boston counterpart, Jim Carey.

The Penguins routinely torched Carey when he played in Washington, but he repeatedly frustrated them last night.

"He played an excellent game," Patrick said. "I thought Mario's line should have had a number of goals, especially early on."

Lemieux drew a hooking penalty from Boston's Jason Allison 53 seconds into the game, and the Penguins capitalized on that power play to take a 1-0 lead.

Beranek got the goal, backhanding a Kevin Hatcher rebound past Carey at 1:08 for his third goal in four games.

Penguins center Petr Nedved got what proved to be the game-winner at 2:52 of the second period. He threw a backhand centering pass toward the front of the net, and the puck deflected off the skate of Boston's Sheldon Kennedy and skidded behind Carey.

The goal was credited to Nedved, his 30th of the season and third in two games.

The Penguins prevented Boston from capitalizing on a holding penalty to Nedved at 16:21, then tried to get Lemieux a goal — he needs one for 50 — when Boston replaced Carey with an extra skater.

But Olczyk ended up scoring almost by accident in the final minute of play, when he lifted a backhander from his own blue line and the puck never stopped until it hit the back of the Boston net.

"If (Lemieux) was open in any way, the puck was going to him," Olczyk said.

Lemieux never got a chance at the empty net, but knew he had not taken advantage of opportunities that had come his way earlier. The problem, he said, was that he simply was pressing in an effort to please the home crowd.

"I think it showed early," Lemieux said. "I was pressing a little too much, rushing my shots. I was a little too nervous."

The fans were more polite than passionate for most of the game, but gave Lemieux several rousing ovations as the third period wound down.

"The crowd was great," Lemieux said. "Especially at the end."

The fans obviously appreciated what Lemieux has meant to the franchise. Heck, even the guys in the other locker room acknowledged the impact he has had.

"What can you say about him?" Bruins coach Steve Kaspar said. "He's a threat every time he's on the ice. He's been a consummate pro ever since he joined Pittsburgh. He's a great player."

LEMIEUX'S LASTING LEGACY

BY GENE COLLIER
Pittsburgh Post-Gazette

A HANDY BAROMETER OF MARIO LEMIEUX'S patience for extended public scrutiny came during the last few minutes before his final regular-season game at the Civic Arena, when 66 and his last teammates queued up along the blue line for the annual team awards ceremony. ¶ Plaques and baubles of all sorts honor everyone from the club's Most Valuable Player (Lemieux) to the Leading Scorer (Lemieux) and include everything from the Booster Club Award (Lemieux) to the Unsung Hero Award (can't be Lemieux because there's still too much singing), to the Good Guy Award, to the Players' Player Award to the Defensive Player of the Year Award to the Rookie of the Year to the Penguin Least Likely To Create A Public Nuisance Trophy.

So as the club extended the proceedings by a minute to present the greatest player in its history a lovely crystal something or other to commemorate his 600th goal, Lemieux let a roaring standing ovation last all of about five seconds before lifting the blade of his stick over his head and saluting the crowd. As Paul Stewart somehow restrained himself from whistling a high-sticking penalty, Lemieux floated out of line and began circling on a purposeful track that screamed, "C'mon, let's play."

"I knew that they wanted to start the game," he said simply.

In his first appearance in uniform since Saturday's final confirmation that this singularly compelling hockey career will end with the close of Penguin post-season business, Lemieux actually appeared a little nervous. He juggled the puck and fired it around more targets than he generally misses in a month.

"I think it showed early that I was pressing too much," he said after snapping off a whopping 11 unsuccessful shots in three periods. Then, with a trace of dejection: "I was rushing my shot."

The Boston Bruins, against whom Lemieux scored the first of 612 career goals some 13 years ago, showed up for this occasion dressed as rotting squash, their hideous sun-dried orange and black uniforms a sweaty metaphor for a wasted season. The Bruins' Jason Allison pulled Lemieux to the ice 53 seconds into the game, and Josef Beranek scored on the Pittsburgh power play only 15 seconds later. The notion that the Bruins might just be mailing this one in, as they had postmarked most of the first 78, had life.

Once Petr Nedved plunked the puck off Sheldon Kennedy on the way to the Boston net halfway through the second period, the name of this game for the rest of the period was strictly get-the-puck-to-the-tall-kid and stand away. In with him two-on-two against Boston goaltender Jim Carey, Stu Barnes almost genuflected to make a pass for an impossible Lemieux shot rather than fire one himself. Jaromir Jagr, on whose shoulders an entire franchise's charisma function will fall within weeks, spent most of the first two periods setting up the man he started collecting posters of as an adolescent in Czechoslovakia. Jagr left late in the period and did not return, apparently as a result of a recurrence of his groin injury.

Lemieux was clearly anxious not only to get his 50th goal of the season, but to hand a standing-room-only crowd something to remember in case the playoffs do not prove terribly memorable.

Few expect the postseason around here to end with Lemieux's soft hands around the Stanley Cup for a third time. His club is too defensively indif-

ferent for that, even if it had the kind of goalkeeping that pushes a hockey club toward June. It doesn't.

Yet when Lemieux finishes, no one will have been cheated. It cost two separate ownership rosters and half a dozen different management models more than $50 million in salary and millions more in medical care for this star-crossed superstar.

And nobody got cheated.

It cost the typical adoring family of four something like $200 every time it wanted to see him skate with a purpose, and still nobody got cheated.

On the core of Lemieux's legacy, you can't put a price, and that was only the complete toxic cleanup of a franchise's massive self-doubt, the magical creation of the wildly exotic idea that the Penguins not only should and would expect success, but have it.

In his first regular season game in this building, Oct. 17, 1984, the place could stage a typical NHL presentation without much need for two-thirds of its seats. He played for an owner, the late Edward J. DeBartolo Sr., who would threaten to move the franchise to Hamilton, Ontario, or at least threaten the people who didn't regard it as a promise.

Now, as we prepare to roll the credits, there are standing-room crowds at up to $85 a ticket, and you are more likely to see hockey played on a Western Pennsylvania street than football or basketball or, don't make me laugh, baseball.

"What can you say about him?" marveled Bruins coach Steve Kasper. "He's a threat every time he's on the ice. He's been a consummate pro ever since he joined Pittsburgh. He's a great player."

Lemieux probably kept his definitive retirement announcement off the record until now to avoid grand tributes in every NHL city, to avoid even the modest events of last night. But it will be many nights, many years, before his name will be anything less than monstrously significant.

Lemieux and his 1996 Hart Trophy.

STATISTICS

1981-82	Laval (QMJHL)
1982-83	Laval (QMJHL)
1983-84	Laval (QMJHL)
1984-85	Pittsburgh (NHL)
1985-86	Pittsburgh (NHL)
1986-87	Pittsburgh (NHL)
1987-88	Pittsburgh (NHL)
1988-89	Pittsburgh (NHL)
1989-90	Pittsburgh (NHL)
1990-91	Pittsburgh (NHL)
1991-92	Pittsburgh (NHL)
1992-93	Pittsburgh (NHL)
1993-94	Pittsburgh (NHL)
1994-95	Pittsburgh (NHL)
1995-96	Pittsburgh (NHL)
1996-97	Pittsburgh (NHL)
RED NUMBERS LED LEAGUE	NHL totals

CALDER TROPHY
NHL Rookie of the Year

'85

ART ROSS TROPHY
NHL's Leading Scorer

'88 '89 '92 '93 '96 '97

LESTER B. PEARSON AWARD
NHL Outstanding Player (Selected by Players)

'86 '88 '93 '96

BILL MASTERTON TROPHY
Perseverance, Sportsmanship and Dedication to Hockey (Selected by NHL)

'93

REGULAR SEASON										PLAYOFFS				
GP	G	A	PTS	PIM	+/–	PP	SH	GW	S	GP	G	A	PTS	PIM
64	30	66	96	22	–	–	–	–	–	18	5	9	14	31
66	84	100	184	76	–	–	–	–	–	12	14	18	32	18
70	133	149	282	92	–	–	–	–	–	14	29	23	52	29
73	43	57	100	54	-35	11	0	0	209	–	–	–	–	–
79	48	93	141	43	-6	17	0	4	276	–	–	–	–	–
63	54	53	107	57	13	19	0	4	267	–	–	–	–	–
77	70	98	168	92	23	22	10	7	382	–	–	–	–	–
76	85	114	199	100	41	31	13	8	313	11	12	7	19	16
59	45	78	123	78	-18	14	3	4	226	–	–	–	–	–
26	19	26	45	30	8	6	1	2	89	23	16	28	44	16
64	44	87	131	94	27	12	4	5	249	15	16	18	34	2
60	69	91	160	38	55	16	6	10	286	11	8	10	18	10
22	17	20	37	32	-2	7	0	4	92	6	4	3	7	2
DID NOT PLAY														
70	69	92	161	54	10	31	8	8	338	18	11	16	27	33
76	50	72	122	65	27	15	2	7	327	5	3	3	6	4
745	613	881	1494	737	151	201	47	65	3054	89	70	85	155	83

HART TROPHY
NHL's Most Valuable Player

'88 '93 '96

CONN SMYTHE TROPHY
NHL Playoffs Most Valuable Player

'91 '92

NHL ALL-STAR
Selected by NHL writers

'86 '87 '88 '89 '91 '93 '96 '97

DAPPER DAN MAN OF THE YEAR
Pittsburgh's Top Athlete

'86 '88

Photographs

PETER DIANA AND THE STAFFS OF THE PITTSBURGH POST-GAZETTE AND THE PITTSBURGH PRESS

COVER, PP. 3, 6-7, 8, 15, 18, 20, 25, 26-7, 29, 31, 36-7, 38, 39, 40, 41, 41, 44-5, 47, 48-9, 50, 51, 52, 59, 63, 64, 65, 66, 70-1, 72, 73, 73, 74, 75, 78, 81, 82, 83, 84, 85, 86-7, 88, 90, 91, 92, 94, 96, 97, 98, 99, 102, 103, 103,107,114, 118, 119, 120, 122, 124, 126, 129, 131, 132, 134, 136, 140, 141, 144, 148, 150, 152, 155, 158-9, 160.

ALLSPORT PHOTOGRAPHY USA

PP. 16, 22-3, 100, 104, 110.

WIDE WORLD PHOTOS

PP. 17, 28, 32, 43, 54-55, 60, 60, 61, 68-9, 77, 106, 108-9, 137, 138-9, 142, 156.

THE GAZETTE (OF MONTREAL)

PP. 9, 11, 46.

CANADIAN PRESS

PP. 12, 42, 58.

His career over, Lemieux hugs Eric Lindros of the Flyers following the Penguins' season-ending loss in the first round of the NHL playoffs.

4.23.97

Pittsburgh Civic Arena

Mario Lemieux leaves the ice after his final home game, a 4-1 playoff victory over the Philadelphia Flyers.